T0080480

WORKPLACE
ETHICS

HarperCollins
LEADERSHIP
An Imprint of HarperCollins

WORKPLACE ETHICS

MASTERING ETHICAL LEADERSHIP
AND SUSTAINING A MORAL WORKPLACE

PAUL FALCONE

© 2022 Paul Falcone

All rights reserved. No portion of this book may be reproduced, stored in a retrieval system, or transmitted in any form or by any means—electronic, mechanical, photocopy, recording, scanning, or other—except for brief quotations in critical reviews or articles, without the prior written permission of the publisher.

Published by HarperCollins Leadership, an imprint of HarperCollins Focus LLC.

Topic 16: From "Attorney-Client Privilege: What You Need to Know." *SHRM HR Daily Newsletter*, March 4, 2020. Copyright 2020 by the Society for Human Resource Management. **Topic 22:** From "Viewpoint: Make This Checklist Your DE&I Launching Point." *SHRM HR Daily Newsletter*, October 5, 2020. Copyright 2020 by the Society for Human Resource Management. **Topic 23:** From "Educate Entry-Level Workers on Workplace Ethics." *SHRM HR Daily Newsletter*, December 6, 2018. Copyright 2018 by the Society for Human Resource Management. All of the above used by permission of the publisher. All rights reserved.

Any internet addresses, phone numbers, or company or product information printed in this book are offered as a resource and are not intended in any way to be or to imply an endorsement by HarperCollins Leadership, nor does HarperCollins Leadership vouch for the existence, content, or services of these sites, phone numbers, companies, or products beyond the life of this book.

This book is written as a source of information only. The information contained in this book should by no means be considered a substitute for the advice, decisions, or judgment of the reader's professional advisors.

All efforts have been made to ensure the accuracy of the information contained in this book as of the date published. The author and the publisher expressly disclaim responsibility for any adverse effects arising from the use or application of the information contained herein.

ISBN 978-1-4002-3007-5 (eBook)
ISBN 978-1-4002-2997-0 (TP)

Library of Congress Control Number: 2021951202

Printed in the United States of America
22 23 24 25 26 LSC 10 9 8 7 6 5 4 3 2 1

CONTENTS

PART 3

INTRODUCTION

It's not always easy to decide between right and wrong at work. Making ethical decisions can help you discern the right thing to do in difficult situations. At its core, ethics is a set of guidelines to help you choose right from wrong. In reality, however, it's so much more than that and has substantial implications in the workplace. For example, ethics drives employee loyalty and engagement as much as it does corporate liability and litigation vulnerability. It's by far the most practical—and interesting—piece of the leadership equation, yet it often gets short shrift in schools, workplaces, and even MBA programs. It's true that business, law, and medical schools require ethics courses and oaths, yet organizations tend to give scant attention in a world changing so quickly from economic, technological, social, scientific, environmental, and business standpoints. Maybe ethics is too time consuming to teach. Maybe it's just too squishy a "soft skill" to invest in. Or perhaps we've simply lost awareness of the basics of ethical business decision-making and accountability because we're moving too quickly as a society and global economy to look back and take a broader overview of the challenges plaguing us.

No matter the reasoning, now is the time to arm your leadership teams and yourself with the tools, wisdom, and stories to help you stand out from your peers and set your leadership brand apart. Make no mistake: there's nothing squishy about ethical decision-making. Organizations that value ethics perform better. If you genuinely want to strengthen the muscle of your frontline operational leadership team, if you want to be identified as an employer of choice, and if you yourself want to develop a reputation as a "favorite boss" and career influencer, start with workplace ethics.

A book of this size logically cannot cover the breadth of ethics in its many forms: environmental sustainability and corporate social responsibility are touched upon, but this book is intended to focus more specifically on workplace ethical dilemmas and internal corporate dynamics that touch your world every day. In many ways, we've lost the ability as a society to sit around the campfire and tell stories and permit the elders to pass on wisdom to the younger generation. Yet here's your chance to create an atmosphere of inclusion, share your hard-won lessons, and make an investment in your people that will provide a handsome personal and organizational return on investment.

Following are some of the practical applications we'll cover in this book:

- Why is it that well-intentioned managers keep stepping on land mines and exposing the organization to liability without even knowing it?
- How do we train our managers to become more adept at sensing when the preemptive strike of "pretaliation" may be lurking? Can employees somehow leverage HR against the company?
- How do organizations with perceived unfair or inconsistent hiring and promotion practices inadvertently suffer from low morale, excessive turnover, and a lack of customer loyalty?
- How do we train our managers to raise their awareness of workplace "fact patterns" that may lend themselves to claims of discrimination, harassment, or retaliation?

▪ How can focusing on creating a more moral and ethical culture help us with hiring, retention, employee development, and employee motivation?

▪ If workers are employed at will, why do we need to issue progressive discipline all the time? And why won't HR let us fire anyone?

▪ What does it mean and how does it apply when we say an organization's code of conduct is about the *spirit* of the law versus the *letter* of the law? Does that somehow give us some greater level of discretion as a management team to address problematic behaviors that may pull down the rest of our team?

▪ Is DEI (diversity, equity, and inclusion) really as critical an imperative as I've heard or is it simply a nice-to-have? And where should we start if we want to transform our organization to become more inclusive and to provide greater equality of opportunity?

▪ How can too much documentation about an employee's poor performance or inappropriate workplace conduct actually hurt our case in court?

▪ Can my company get sued for *non*sexual harassment? Can I get sued personally?

▪ How can I encourage my organization to become more socially aware of its moral obligations to environmental sustainability and social responsibility?

And there's a lot more to workplace ethics that you're going to want to gear up for. Corporate America is experiencing evolutionary change at revolutionary speed. Arguably, the workplace is changing faster now than at any time in history. You'll want to ensure that you're staying informed of the changes resulting from artificial intelligence (AI), for example, since that will affect every aspect of your employee hiring, retention, training, and turnover practices as well as your customers' buying behaviors. But algorithms and analytics can skew reality if not observed closely, creating tremendous ethical—and potentially unlawful—consequences for the unsuspecting or inattentive organization.

You need this book to align your leadership teams, to encourage everyone to become more aware of the ethical and moral implications of their decisions, and to focus their energies on fostering a healthy workplace culture. And the advice needs to be practical, easy to understand, and flexible enough to accommodate your organization's changing needs. In short, you'll want a resource that helps you establish an ethics baseline that all leaders and employees can adhere to, not because they have to but because they want to. It's not as hard as you think. You simply have to model the behaviors, provide the right tools, and encourage your frontline leaders to communicate and apply them. Welcome to step 1 of reinventing your culture, becoming an employer of choice, and reenergizing your workforce by incentivizing the right behaviors to benefit your organization, your employees, customers, and your community as a whole. Good corporate citizenship starts right here and right now. I'm so looking forward to joining you on this journey!

PART
1

OUR HISTORY, OUR LAWS, AND OUR EVOLVING WORKPLACE

WHAT IS WORKPLACE ETHICS
ALL ABOUT AND WHY THIS BOOK?

Workplace ethics represents the consummate body of knowledge that impacts and influences daily business decision-making and the strategic trajectory of your organization. Sound important enough and did I get your attention? But it's about more than just knowledge: it's about wisdom. Wisdom is knowledge applied. Passing along workplace wisdom is something woefully lacking in today's day and age. Why? Likely because we're moving too quickly and not communicating enough. Therefore, it's critical that you—the senior executive, business owner, or frontline manager—take the time to pass down hard-won wisdom to those who look up to you and depend on you for their own future career growth.

Think about it: Doesn't it make sense to establish your values and philosophy for all new hires *before* they launch into their new careers at your organization? Wouldn't you prefer a workplace free of angst and drama, one where people have each other's backs and can do their best work every day, free from that walking-on-eggshells feeling or those little indiscretions that chip away at people's self-confidence or sense of self-worth? It's definitely doable if you make room for it. Instilling a greater sense of purpose and accountability in all of your employees is a core goal that you can commit to achieving in one quarter or one year, depending how you choose to define and measure it. And wouldn't it be ideal if a simple, short book could reengage your leadership team to reinvent itself and pass along newfound wisdom to staff members? Look no further: the tool is here, right in your hands. Let's get started and bring you up to speed with some of the most interesting and fascinating aspects of history, employment law, and ethics that will help your frontline operational leaders think more wisely before they act.

Ethics is important because sometimes it isn't easy to decide what is right and what is wrong. Many of the choices you will have to make in your workplace will be unclear or complicated. The good news is that using ethics will help you make better choices in all types of situations.

Ethics define what is morally right or wrong.

First, some definitions:

■ **Ethics.** A code of moral standards by which people judge the actions and behaviors of themselves and others.
■ **Business Ethics.** The application of ethics to business and business practices. This includes the study of organizations and the historical, ethical decisions they've made. The aim of business ethics is to do the right thing and build a great business by doing so in a spirit of profit through purpose.
■ **Workplace Ethics.** The application of an ethical code of conduct to the operational and strategic management of an organization and its leadership and people practices.
■ **Ethics Versus Morals.** Please note that this book uses the words *ethics* and *morals* interchangeably. Of course, there can

be a difference: someone without a moral compass may follow ethical codes to remain in good standing with society out of a sense of compliance. In comparison, someone may violate ethical codes because they believe they are doing something morally right out of principle. For practical purposes and so as not to cause any confusion, we will use the words *ethical* and *moral* as synonyms, meaning basically the same thing.

Ethical and moral considerations should drive every business's decision-making and operations. But we continue to see ethical challenges and lapses in judgment in the business world, sports, entertainment, politics, the sciences, and just about every other human endeavor. Sure, it sounds like a high bar to reach, and make no mistake: it can be, especially when trying to turn around a culture that tolerates lax ethical behaviors. But a consistently ethical culture is habit forming and easier to sustain than you might otherwise think. The goal, therefore, is to allow the space to groove new neural pathways that make expectations of ethically responsible behavior the norm.

It's all about building muscle around the situational thinking that drives your company's daily operations and long-term planning. Like any muscle, it gets stronger when measured and developed, but it can likewise atrophy if it's simply a statement or a policy that gathers dust in a company handbook or policy and procedure manual. This is real. It's alive. It should be present in all you do and become a part of who you are as an organization and as a leadership team. It should become a core competency on your annual performance review template in addition to a key element of your bonus programs. And it needs to become part of your organization's parlance and lexicon from this day forward. Let this become the "Good Book" that your executives, managers, and supervisors rely on and refer to in charting the course for your organization's future.

THE FOUNDATION

LEGAL VERSUS ETHICAL STANDARDS

I f you're a history buff or a philosopher, if you enjoy employment law or simply have an interest in how to drive higher organizational and individual performance, you'll enjoy the road we're about to explore together. First, let's distinguish between legal and ethical standards to appreciate their differences:

- **Legal Standard.** A focus on compliance and the avoidance of wrongdoing that could run afoul of the law; the underlying question is, "*Can* I do this?"
- **Ethical Standard.** Building a moral corporate culture based on authenticity, integrity, and transparency; the underlying question is, "*Should* I do this?"

Put another way, *legal* means within the law, while *ethical* means doing the right thing. Here's the rub: the law often lags behind ethical standards, so you won't want "what's legal" to serve as the primary driver of your decision-making. In other words, a company that merely complies with the law can end up with gaping holes in its responsibilities to its employees, customers, and community as a whole, simply because there hasn't been enough time for the law to catch up to the unethical (and potentially illegal) practices.

For example, government regulators arguably didn't know about the cancer-causing properties of tobacco or asbestos for years; later litigation showed that senior management knew of the dangers posed by their products, yet decades went by before criminal exposure resulted. But because government regulators claimed they didn't know that those products were unsafe at the time, it hadn't produced regulations to require that those manufacturing companies make safer products, alter their production standards, or cease production altogether. The companies continued to produce cancer-causing products because it wasn't *against the law* to do so, although hindsight tells us that these organizations were highly unethical for covering up such critical—and deadly—data.

Both legal and ethical considerations are clearly important, but which one rings truer to you, grabs your attention, and feels like something you want to strive for? If you're like most, it's clearly the ethical standard. That's where you want to be at all times. The legal standard is simply the low bar—the lowest common denominator— that distinguishes lawfulness from unlawfulness (such as criminal damages, civil liability, and the like). Rarely will that excite anyone unless they're concerned about going to jail (and we'll assume that's not the case here!). But that's a reality of the ethics world too. As we'll learn when we read about the Sarbanes-Oxley Act, or SOX, real-world penalties of jail time and multimillion-dollar *individual* fines come into play in matters of defective certification and willful noncompliance. (Believe me, they don't pay you enough money to risk going to jail and losing all your assets for messing with the books of your corporation's financial statements!)

No, the driver that tugs at your heart will always focus on building a moral culture, an organization in which people can do their best work every day, feel respected and empowered, and perform at a higher level because they're self-motivated and highly engaged. It's exactly that level of discretionary effort that drives innovation and creativity, that links people's performance at work to the achievements and accomplishments that they can profile on their own annual self-reviews, resumes, and LinkedIn profiles, and that makes the employment experience a win-win for company and worker alike. True, there's no job great enough for the human spirit. But you know when you're rocking it, when you and your people are fully engaged, when you're hitting home runs and getting the recognition and appreciation you feel you deserve. More likely than not, those circumstances occur when you have a great relationship with your own boss, when you're fully engaged and tied into your company's mission and goals, and when you've got the right team in place to build upon one another's talents and have fun all at the same time.

When those elements are present, when the energy of the team comes together and creates an output that far exceeds the contributions of the individual players, and when the achievements flow easily because you've aligned your organization's needs with your employees' career interests and professional goals, you've got nowhere to go but up. One of the fundamental underlying elements in situations like these stems from your commitment to workplace ethics and inclusion. This doesn't have to be a once-in-a-career opportunity: you can replicate it wherever you go. And remember, the greatest leaders are not those with the most followers; they're the ones who create the most leaders in turn. Authenticity, integrity, and transparency are the starting points in determining who you are and who you choose to be. From that starting point, you'll naturally do the things that make you a great boss and a great company. Never lose sight of the basics and return to them often: they won't let you down.

3

GAINING AN UNDERSTANDING OF THE ETHICAL CHALLENGES YOU MAY FACE ON A PRACTICAL BASIS AS A BUSINESS PROFESSIONAL

We often hear and interchange the words *ethical* or *moral* and think of the very high-level impact of their implications: insider trading, sexual misconduct, harassment, financial fraud, and the like make headlines daily. Of course, those make up part of the equation, but violations of ethical standards in the workplace probably happen every day on a lesser scale (think taking home office supplies or calling in sick around the holidays). Day-to-day operational and people decisions hinge on each leader's awareness of the conduct and behavioral standards that create your organization's internal culture and external reputation.

There are so many ways to be successful *through* people, and no leader or executive wants to be successful *despite* people. But how do you strengthen that natural desire to become someone's favorite boss, someone they look up to and thank decades later for making them the successful person they've become? Interestingly enough, it's in many of the smallest and most routine things you do. On the one hand, do you display role-model behavior when it comes to treating people fairly and respectfully, acting with integrity, making your word your bond, and teaching those who follow in your footsteps to do the same? On the other, do you make it safe for your people to trust you, to feel comfortable making themselves vulnerable to you, and to be willing to share with you their career needs and true longer-term professional interests (even if it means potentially exploring new opportunities at other companies)?

Getting down into the weeds a bit further, give some thought to how you might respond to the following on-the-spot, watercooler types of one-off questions from members of your team or employees from other departments:

"Jack, can I talk to you off the record for a minute?"

"Sam, I can't talk to my boss about something that's really bothering me. I know you're her peer and I sense that you're good friends. Would you mind if I picked your brain for a few minutes to get your advice on how to work with her better?"

"Nina, I really didn't want to say anything, and please don't use my name here, but it looks like Ashley's been hitting on Mike pretty heavily, and he told me he's definitely not happy with his boss constantly asking him out to dinner and badgering him. We're all starting to notice it now."

"Anthony, this company is so cheap. They never invest in any of the latest technology. They always say they're broke unless someone gives notice: then they find money out of nowhere to entice the person to stay by making a counteroffer. Do you really have to quit around here to get noticed and get a raise?"

And the list goes on. Any one of these real-life scenarios can pop up at you out of nowhere, and your automatic, gut-level initial response has more ethical implications than you might otherwise think. We'll examine these very types of conundrums throughout the book, keeping a keen eye on the moral as well as legal considerations that should factor into your responses.

For now, let's start with a practical piece of wisdom you can share with your staffers as they grow and excel in their careers: *Change your perspective and you'll change your perception.* Help your employees—especially when they're frustrated—get out of the weeds and have a look at the situation from the thirty-thousand-foot level. Try saying something like:

■ Looking at this as objectively as you can, why do you think this may have developed over the past few months, and what can we do now to remedy it? More important, what role do you want to play in the resolution?

■ I want to hear your evaluation and analysis of this. Being as objective as you can to both sides of the argument, tell me why you feel that may have happened or why they might feel that way?

■ Can I share with you what this looks like from my vantage point?

■ What suggestions do you have for becoming a better mentor and coach for these two individuals, and how can you hold them to a greater level of accountability?

■ I know that perception is reality until proven otherwise. It looks to me like you may have a perception-management problem on your hands, and I'm happy to help you with that. Let's talk about what may have led to this and how we can fix it together.

■ I understand that you may be under a lot of pressure right now. But that doesn't excuse behavior that could make others feel uncomfortable, ill at ease, or otherwise put down or humiliated in front of their peers. You're responsible just like I am for creating a friendly and inclusive working environment. And I have to hold you to the same standard that I hold myself and everyone else on the team to. What do you think might be your best approach to addressing the blowup that just happened on the sales floor?

■ What can we use as "feed forward" for the rest of the team to avoid these types of miscommunications or mistaken assumptions again in the future?

Yes, situations that require these types of responses are all ethical realities that will challenge you in the workplace on any given day. Your fundamental question will always be: Who are you in light of these challenges and whom do you choose to be? Are you someone who shies away from conflict? Do you tend to sweep things under the rug and hope they fix themselves? Are you willing to bond conflictive teams or groups? Can you commit to "constructive confrontation" by employing a coaching and mentoring approach toward conflict resolution? Will you have your people's backs when necessary but also hold them accountable to the highest standards, when needed? Ah, you're starting to see that ethical leadership takes on many styles, shapes, and forms.

Look at the definition of ethics again:

A code of moral standards by which people judge the actions and behaviors of themselves and others

Such moral standards reveal themselves in the smallest—yet most impactful—ways. And remember this: *beingness trumps doingness.* Who you are is far more critical than what you do. Always focus on who you are being in any given situation—your character, the way you treat others, the dignity and respect you bestow upon others, and the degree to which you will permit others to make themselves vulnerable to you (which stems from trust). After all, who you are triggers everything you do, not vice versa.

Finally, remember the adage, *what you want for yourself, give to another.* That simple injunction will help guide you as a leader throughout your career. You're responsible for the workplace experience that your team enjoys. As a leader in corporate America, you create the sense of teamwork, camaraderie, and respect that those you lead get to experience. No excuses: no matter how many bullets are flying over your head or who's yelling and screaming above you, your job is to protect your team members from that craziness and create your own "miniculture" of sorts in your department or team that reflects your values and ethics. Ask yourself: Would you want to work for you? If everyone in the company followed your lead, would you be happy with where you took it?

You play a vital role in ensuring the effectiveness of your organization's compliance efforts. Your day-to-day responsibilities must include compliance with legal requirements and ethical principles. Always be on the lookout for noncompliance. If you see something that is not right, report it! Make sure that you are familiar with your organization's policies and procedures regarding legal and ethical conduct. Recognize your responsibility in making sure your compliance program is successful.

A WORD TO THE WISE

Whenever possible, include others when making ethical decisions and share final decisions publicly when appropriate to do so. Diverse interests and perspectives usually improve decision-making, and the decision process is likely deemed credible and fair by the court of public opinion when not handled by only one individual. It is always a best practice to avoid any suspicion of unfair bias.

A BRIEF OVERVIEW OF THE STUDY OF ETHICS

A STARTING PLACE

This book is not intended to spend much time wading through theory. When it comes to ethics—a branch of philosophy that distinguishes between right and wrong and the moral consequences of human actions—there are histories and theories galore, from Plato and Aristotle to John Locke, Thomas Hobbes, Thomas Aquinas, and Immanuel Kant. But you can't really read a book on ethics without a basic grounding on the fundamentals—even a short overview will do. With that spirit in mind, let's go over the basics of the study and discipline of ethics and how humankind has grappled with doing what's right, doing the right thing, and how to arrive at the optimal solution.

We know that what constitutes right and wrong changes across time and across societies. There are three main categories of ethical studies that will help you:

Metaethics. Focuses on the terms, definitions, and parameters that people use to define right and wrong and good and bad and how to determine what's appropriate. The most abstract area of the ethics universe, metaethics looks to explore whether morality is subjective or objective, how what's deemed good or bad depends on the individual's points of view, and whether someone can truly know what is absolutely right or wrong.

Descriptive Ethics. Attempts to describe a group's or society's ethical views and values as to what is bad or good, how beliefs influence actions, and how different societies reward or punish based on their present understanding of right and wrong (that is, moral or immoral).

Normative Ethics. Aims at providing a justified basis for how people should conduct their lives. Unlike descriptive ethics, which focuses on what people may believe is right or wrong at any given time, normative ethics focuses on how to live a moral life at a higher and purer level.

Further, ethical theories break down how people should respond according to one of three main theories above: the character of the person performing the action (virtue ethics); the basis or justification for ethical action (deontological ethics), or the results of the action (consequential ethics). As you might guess, depending on what's being studied—war, the Holocaust, pandemics, or large versus small government—various aspects of ethics may apply.

Virtue ethics, for example, focuses on moral traits rather than societal obligations or the consequences of one's action. Virtue ethics look to "doing the right thing" and "being good" under *all* circumstances, regardless of other considerations. Should this rule in all circumstances? After all, virtuous habits like truthfulness, fairness, justice, and integrity should trump all else, right? Or would it be naive to look solely to virtue ethics to drive decisions and actions in the real world? Maybe deontological ethics makes more sense in the workplace as a more practical and workable theory. After all, the word *deontology* stems from the Greek word for "duty" or "obligation." Should duty and obligation determine the optimal ethical construct for today's workplace? Better yet, should the consequences of one's actions (that is, the ethical theory of consequentialism) apply here, seeing that acts themselves aren't good or bad—they're only deemed good or bad based on what happens because of them?

This drills down even further: *Ethical egoism* states that being a moral person means acting in your own best interests. *Ethical altruism* argues that moral people are obligated to act in the best interests of others. *Utilitarianism* focuses strictly on what creates the greatest good for the largest number of people, considering the effects and consequences of your actions on the largest number of people. *Hedonism* posits that pleasure is the only thing that's inherently good, while *welfarism* focuses on the greatest good for the greatest number of people. But wait, there's more! *Situational ethics* is a new entrant into the ethics pool (think 1960s) that focuses on agape, or absolute, unchanging, and unconditional love for all people under all circumstances.

If you're getting a feel for the vastness of the struggle, the myriad influences over time that can give rise to new theories of ethics, and the circumstances and conditions that may change as people's views are altered, you'll see why most business ethicists agree that no one theory works in every business or in every business situation. After all, each ethical theory has its own strengths, weaknesses, and applicability to specific circumstances. As an operational leader or human resources practitioner in the twenty-first century, you'll likely find your ethical balance somewhere between:

- Virtue ethics, which focus on the character of an ethical leader or ethical employee
- Deontological efforts, which focus on duty to self and others (that is, duty to the company)
- Utilitarianism, which promotes practicality and the greatest good for everyone involved

Just mention one of these three ethical constructs if your boss asks you if you read this book and what you got out of it. You'll garner all the requisite oohs and aahs for having studied such a noble subject with such big words!

5

ETHICS PROGRAMS AVAILABLE
IN TODAY'S WORKPLACE

NOT NEARLY ENOUGH TO SOLVE ALL YOUR
PROBLEMS—UNLESS YOU MAKE IT PERSONAL

You may be thinking, why all this fuss about ethics? We've already got our compliance programs in place. Well, while existing programs may be helpful, most organizations would likely argue that they aren't enough. And they would be correct. Following are the three types of programs you may be familiar with:

- Codes and compliance programs (e.g., SOX, ISO) focus on preventing unwanted unethical or unlawful behaviors.
- Corporate identity and values programs focus on what a company stands for and the good qualities the company wants its employees to exhibit.
- Social outreach programs focus on corporate social responsibility and the idea of tying the company's products and services to the broader good of helping others socially, economically, and environmentally.

In addition, diversity, equity, and inclusion (DEI) awareness training and racial justice initiatives are accompanying movements, like Women in Leadership and Gender Pay Equity, to create a more balanced and sustainable workplace, including at the corporate board level.

Looking at these titles and the broad swath of areas they cover, what could possibly be missing from corporate compliance programs? The answer: Ethics at the individual level. Ethics as a fundamental and core element of corporate culture. Ethics as a tool to hire, develop, and retain top talent. And yes—ethics to hold people to a higher standard of performance and accountability. In short, the programs above, while excellent in design and intent, aren't necessarily personal. They're *programs*. They're *initiatives*. Corporate compliance programs help organizations prevent, detect, and correct unlawful and unethical conduct. They represent corporate goals and values, and rightfully so: every company is a corporate citizen, obligated to not just turn a profit but to make the community and environment a better place. But until those core values are fostered by the leader and adopted by each employee, workers may miss the personal experience of being part of a *culture* that emanates fairness and inclusion, transparency and trust, respect and, yes, love.

Corporate compliance programs help ensure that employees do not violate the law and therefore benefit organizations by:

■ Providing concrete demonstration that your organization is committed to ethical corporate conduct

■ Increasing the likelihood of identifying and preventing unethical or unlawful conduct

■ Prompting employees to be vigilant for compliance violations

> ■ Providing a mechanism to encourage employees to report potential problems and allow for appropriate internal inquiry and corrective actions
> ■ Helping reduce employees' and the organization's exposure to civil damages, penalties, and criminal sanctions

Only when workplace ethics become part of your corporate fabric, your personal and collective values, and your cultural DNA will they resonate with your employees, customers, and other stakeholders. If you truly value fairness, inclusion, integrity, and team alignment, you'll get there much faster by making ethics a part of your vocabulary, your daily lexicon, your written word, and your shared discussions. What's needed in many organizations is a shift in consciousness, a change in awareness, and a renewed respect for one another. You won't get there by wishing for it. And you can't wait for anyone else to start. This is your company and your career, and you are paying it forward to those whom you have the privilege of leading and influencing. Focusing on ethics in all its manifestations will get you where you want to go faster than just about anything else.

SPECIAL TIP: EXPRESS THIS ON DAY ONE.
HERE'S WHAT IT LOOKS LIKE WHEN IT WORKS . . .

I was fortunate enough to serve as head of human resources for the Nickelodeon Animation Studio in Burbank, California. I transferred to Nickelodeon after a number of years at its sister company, Paramount Pictures. Mark Taylor, Nickelodeon's senior vice president and general manager, was likely the greatest leader I've ever worked for. Mark is one of the nicest people you'll ever meet, but he brought Nickelodeon to a level of success where they became the number one children's cable TV network—even over Disney—during his reign. Mark knew all five hundred employees by name, he practiced MBWA—management by walking around—was visible, maintained an open-door policy, knew the business inside and out, and made Nickelodeon the number one destination where animators wanted to work. *SpongeBob SquarePants, Dora the Explorer, Avatar,* and many other high-profile animation productions were humming away under the humble roof of that small studio on a nondescript corner across from the train tracks in that downtown Burbank neighborhood.

What Mark did especially well, however, occurred during new employees' first week. Once a month when we held new employee orientation, Mark scheduled about an hour to meet with each cohort of new hires in the main conference room. He wanted to know them personally, make sure they found in one another a special bond as new hires, and used the opportunity to share "Mark's Big 8 Rules of the Road." He shared how special the Nickelodeon family was and how he held each new hire accountable for perpetuating the culture that was so dear to him and everyone else. His "Big 8" focused on high quality, personal accountability, mutual respect, and passion for your work. He included the importance of "true leadership," whether you were in management or in an individual contributor role. And he handed out a values sheet with those principles and mantras mapped out, with the byline:

Strong Principles + Belief in People = Strong Leadership

Mark was and still is an animation industry legend. How exciting for new hires—from animators to accountants to mail room staff and janitors—to spend time with him, feel his genuine concern for them and the organization, and assume responsibility for making his priorities theirs. But wait, there's more! If the large group orientation took place on Monday, a follow-up meeting on Wednesday occurred for anyone who was responsible for supervising people. Mark again had the opportunity to discuss the values sheet, this time focusing on his expectations of these new leaders in terms of communication, teambuilding, and becoming a great leadership team. With this opportunity, however, he also focused on the negative consequences for not meeting these expectations and shared how he held the management team to a higher standard of accountability than everyone else.

There was no doubt about it: everyone understood the culture that was so safely cherished, the values of the GM, and the expectations going forward in terms of performance, productivity, respect, and gratitude. Oh yes, and there was always that eighth and final principle: fun. Granted, this was an animation studio, and most organizations won't have as much discretion in implementing fun and creative activities like Nickelodeon, but Mark was a prankster. He kept the nerf guns in his office, arranged the holiday theme parties, and tried to outdo himself every year. As an HR professional, I could only sit back and watch in amazement as everything I wrote about in my books and taught in my UCLA Extension courses came to life before my very eyes.

If you're a CEO, business owner, division or department head, or supervisor or team lead, share your values and your expectations up front and openly. State them proudly, give examples of how they work, and remind everyone that your culture is unique and worthy of attention. Add a permanent topical point to your staff meetings and employee gatherings, asking for recent examples that further your organization's mission and values. Celebrate success. Lighten up and have fun, to the degree you can and that would be appropriate. Know that people will feel more secure when they understand what's expected of them, when they can relate to you and your values as their leader, and when they appreciate the opportunity to join and remain part of a special family. Nickelodeon's success soared under Mark Taylor's leadership; tell your story about your history and culture proudly, set expectations, and raise the bar for all employees to perform at their highest level. It begins on day one. It's amazing how a simple philosophy—clearly expressed and modeled every day—can have such a tremendous impact on an organization. Great leadership can be yours: all it takes is a change to your fundamental thought about who you are and who you choose to be.

6

ETHICS AND CULTURE

THE CORE COMPONENT OF YOUR
HUMAN CAPITAL STRATEGY

anagement guru Peter Drucker famously said, "Culture eats strategy for breakfast." What he meant by those words of wisdom was that no matter how brilliant your strategy, how precise your operating plan, or how clear your organizational goals, if your culture isn't aligned properly and functioning at a high level, little will come of your efforts. A house divided will not stand. In short, a powerful and empowering culture is a surer route to organizational success than just about anything else.

Corporate culture affects every aspect of human capital strategy from the organization's recruitment and selection efforts to performance management, compensation, employee development, and liability management. Your people define your culture, and your frontline operational leadership team exhibits your organization's moral values every day in terms of communication, teambuilding, conflict resolution, and employee recognition and engagement. If you think of culture as the oil running through your car, you can quickly visualize why you may get very different results putting your foot on the gas (marketing and sales) or brakes (finance and compliance), depending on what's going on in the internal, behind-the-scenes efficiency of the engine.

A healthy culture thrives on trust. Honesty is at the heart of every code of conduct. Always be truthful in your communications and conduct. Happy employees make for productive workers in terms of going the extra mile and exercising greater discretionary effort. And productive workers will typically rate their organization very highly on surveys that ask the simple questions "Are you able to do your best work every day?" and "Do you trust management?" Documenting your organization's values of integrity, respect, commitment, and accountability, for example, is a great place to start, but vocalizing your mission at the beginning of large gatherings is even more important. Asking employees to share examples of your corporate mission in action keeps it alive and thriving. Leading by example should be every operational manager's responsibility, one that gets measured and managed as part of their annual performance review and merit increase or bonus award.

Reinforcing and internalizing your mission and values helps it become part of your organizational DNA. How else do you strengthen and enforce ethical values? Train managers and employees annually on the code of conduct and remind them of your expectations. Tell stories and share examples of your cultural values by sponsoring employee volunteer events, enacting employee recognition programs, launching employee benevolence programs (for example, permitting employees to donate a certain amount of their vacation pay to coworkers in need), earmarking corporate matching funds for selected nonprofits, introducing peer recognition programs (especially for employees who work remotely and sometimes feel disconnected from the larger team), measuring and strengthening your internal promotion rate, and evaluating how you're doing with the help of employee satisfaction surveys, focus groups, and exit interview feedback.

Make it fun and keep it light. Strive to achieve buy-in at all levels of the organization. Hang posters. Place ethics and integrity highlights on the main page of your intranet site. Create space for ethics, recognition, and inclusion to thrive. But know one thing: when your organization is described by your employees using terms like *ethical, moral, fair, consistent, encouraging, sincere, honest, inclusive,* and *selfless,* your strategic objectives and goals will have a much greater chance of being attained and even exceeded. The opposite is also true, especially with career websites like Glassdoor and Comparably constantly eliciting feedback from current and former employees. You shouldn't need a reputation management firm to help you undo bad publicity; you simply need to create an ethical and inclusive work environment where employees can do their best work every day and find new ways of reinventing themselves in light of your organization's changing needs.

When is the last time you added a new values-in-action program to recognize and reward ethical behavior or that reflects your organization's mission and values? When is the last time you've spoken about or shared examples of them? Have you elicited feedback from your employees recently about what they'd like to see that connects their daily work to a greater social cause or that would help them do their best work every day or avoid burnout? Likewise, have you created clearly defined pathways for career advancement, making job roles a journey rather than a dead end? Remember that this doesn't have to be a perfect start; it just has to start. Aligning an individual's intrinsic motivators with an organization's extrinsic motivators remains the ultimate goal in professional and career development. So, go ahead: You be the first domino. You model the change that you want to see in others. Live the reality you wish to experience, beginning now. From there, culture, self-motivation, and performance and productivity will naturally fall into place and take care of themselves.

OVERCOMING ETHICAL OBSTACLES (COMMON WORKPLACE ETHICS MYTHS)

It's easy to make excuses and fool yourself into justifying actions that aren't ethical. Common obstacles include:

- "There's no other choice" (the necessity obstacle). The best way to overcome this obstacle is by spreading the benefits to others.
- "It won't matter; just this once" (the no consequences obstacle). The optimal way of overcoming this obstacle is by spreading the costs: small costs can add up over time and have significant consequence.
- "There's no law against it" (the permissibility obstacle). Overcome this by respecting rights. Think about the people who will be affected by your decision.
- "I deserve this" (the entitlement obstacle)—tricking yourself into thinking you're righting a wrong. Overcome this by reversing assumptions: How would you feel if the tables were turned? Would you still feel your decision is ethical?

To remove obstacles to ethical decision-making, analyze the costs and benefits, not just to yourself but to everyone potentially affected. Ask yourself if everyone is being treated with respect and fairness.

SOX COMPLIANCE, ANTIHARASSMENT, AND EFFECTIVE INTERNAL INVESTIGATIONS

THE SARBANES-OXLEY ACT OF 2002

WHERE THE RUBBER MEETS THE ROAD

Sarbanes-Oxley Act = reforms in corporate governance
The goal = transparency to investors

At the beginning of the twenty-first century, much was amiss in corporate America. The late 1990s witnessed a stock market run full of incredible potential based on a new economic model using something called the "internet." "Dot-coms" flooded the market with new ways of selling goods directly to consumers without the need for brick-and-mortar storefronts or customer service staffers. And investors ate up these opportunities coming their way in the form of IPOs—initial public offerings—through which they invested their hard-earned money in good faith based on the economic potential of startups, many of which would soon crash due to unsustainable business models. Against that backdrop, we can add enormous conflicts of interest that led to devastating business failures in the early 2000s:

■ Relationships between businesses and the accounting firms they hired blurred the lines that were supposed to protect the investing public. For example, large public accounting firms offered accounting, audit, and *consulting services* to their clients, making it difficult (if not impossible) for them to provide an impartial evaluation of their clients' financial status. After all, public accounting firms had split obligations, both to their clients and to the public. But which should win out in the absence of clear guidance?

■ Investment banks on Wall Street financing mergers and stock offerings had a vested interest in their client company's share price, which compromised the "honest and objective assessments" they were supposed to provide to the investing public. Instead of fulfilling their ethical and fiduciary obligations, many insiders advanced their own self-interests (called self-dealing) at the expense of those whose interests they were responsible for protecting.

■ A spate of high-profile business failings littered the headlines: Enron, WorldCom, Tyco International, and Arthur Andersen— behemoths of corporate America—imploded, revealing unethical business practices and conflicts of interest galore.

Such very public business scandals and economic crises shone a bright light on everything from insider trading to embezzlement, from CEO incentives to auditor-audited conflicts of interest, and from product safety to safety in the workplace. In short, with the passage of the Sarbanes-Oxley Act of 2002, or SOX, as it is often abbreviated, Congress demanded more accountability, responsibility, and more morally acceptable behavior from publicly traded corporations. Before long, privately held companies adopted their own SOX-inspired codes of conduct and other corporate governance practices—even though they weren't legally obligated to do so—because the concept made so much sense as an overarching approach to ethical and moral business practices.

Further, when Congress passed the act, the new law unleashed an array of corporate obligations and responsibilities, not the least of which affected the day-to-day conduct of employees of publicly traded companies. When most US workers hear the name Sarbanes-Oxley, the first thing that comes to mind is financial and operational controls and disclosure requirements. And while financial measures and reforms in corporate governance standards make up a majority of SOX initiatives, documented codes of ethics are also a mainstay of the act. To comply with the new law, publicly traded companies must disclose whether they have a code of ethics, and if they do not, they have to explain why. This code of ethics, often referred to as a business conduct statement, must be proactively communicated to all employees. In fact, effective SOX ethics and compliance training is a mitigating factor in federal criminal sentencing guidelines in the event a corporate official or the organization itself finds itself in hot water facing a criminal conviction.

That "proactive communication" typically comes in the form of live or online training, and here's why it's so critical: when SOX was passed, it had teeth. After the great stock market crash of 2000–03, when millions of investors lost billions of dollars in the equities market, many having depended in good faith on falsified corporate financial statements, Congress made sure that any public companies that failed to comply with SOX reporting requirements would face stiff consequences:

- Specifically, CEOs and CFOs could face penalties of up to $1 million and/or imprisonment for up to ten years for something known as "defective certification." Defective certification means that the corporate official either knew or should have known about inaccuracies in the company's filed financial statements but failed to correct them. (In other words, they did not submit the defective financial statement by mistake or accident.)

■ In addition, CEOs and CFOs could face penalties of up to $5 million and/or imprisonment for up to twenty years for "willful noncompliance" or fraud (meaning that the corporate official certified the defective financial statement voluntarily and intentionally, knowing that his or her conduct was illegal). With CEOs and CFOs now criminally liable, American corporations no doubt took notice and rolled out ethics and compliance programs in all worldwide locations at an unprecedented pace.

SOX was a game changer in 2002 in terms of reestablishing the need for ethics and morals as part of every publicly traded company's DNA. Unfortunately, when regulations get lax, people find ways of exploiting loopholes in the law to their own advantage, and the next massive crash came just six years later in 2008 with the mortgage meltdown and Great Recession. The 2008 financial crisis was yet again rife with conflicts of interest, many of which involved self-dealing. For example, the investment banking firm Goldman Sachs sold mortgage debt to its client Washington Mutual Bank. Then Goldman Sachs shorted Washington Mutual stock because Goldman believed that the mortgage debt was shaky. As a result, Washington Mutual stock plummeted, and the company collapsed in September 2008. Yet Goldman Sachs made millions on its short sale. The lesson? There is a definite need for government regulation of the private sector. How much is required, how much is too much, and how to protect investors' investments will always remain a challenge and an argument. But make no mistake about it: Sarbanes-Oxley remains a critical piece of the regulatory puzzle and plays a significant role in financial disclosure, transparency, and stomping out conflicts of interest.

8

YOUR KEY SOX OBLIGATION

DISCLOSE POTENTIAL CONFLICTS OF INTEREST

Let's first look at your obligations to your company. SOX contains management certification requirements that confirm that no potential conflicts of interest exist that could threaten the validity of a corporate filing. To avoid defective certification, a CEO must certify that the information contained in a financial report like a 10Q (quarterly report) or 10K (annual report) is accurate and complete. And the only way your CEO can do that is to poll the workforce and ask employees to certify that they in turn have no conflicts of interest that could interfere with the larger corporate filing. (Remember, it was the decision of only a handful of Enron executives and Chicago-based Arthur Andersen auditors shredding documents in the basement of Enron's headquarters in Houston that brought down both organizations!)

So, what does a potential conflict of interest look like? Put simply:

A conflict of interest is simply a situation in which you have competing interests that can interfere with your obligations toward your employer. A conflict potentially exists when your outside business or personal interests adversely affect or have the appearance of adversely affecting your judgment at work.

It's critical that you disclose in writing anything that could place your company at risk, and having an undisclosed family relationship with coworkers, customers, suppliers, or competitors of the company is typically the number one issue. Other examples of potential conflicts include:

- Accepting a personal benefit that obligates you in any way to a customer, vendor, or competitor
- Accepting or offering cash under any circumstances
- Taking a business opportunity away from your company by doing personal business with a customer, supplier, or competitor of the company, except as a regular consumer
- Having a financial interest in a customer, supplier, or competitor, other than less than 1 percent ownership of a publicly traded company

How do you handle such situations? Simply report these potential conflicts on any employee certification form that your company asks you to complete. To be on the safe side, even if you're not given a formal disclosure form, email the issue to your supervisor so that you have an electronic record of the disclosure to protect yourself. This is particularly true if you are in a "position of trust," meaning that you are required to exercise good judgment in your service to your organization. Conflicts of interest come in a variety of forms, of course, and arguably all employees are in a position of trust to some degree. Just remember that conflicts of interest place a conflict between your own self-interests and the interests of the organization you serve. In most cases, conflicts don't result in un-ethical behavior. But conflicts have been known to nudge people over the border line into unethical and even criminal territory. Hence, organizations typically take a "full disclosure / total transparency" approach to any potential conflicts of interest. Openness and transparency are key: deals that take place behind closed doors and that aren't subject to scrutiny are far more likely to breach ethical boundaries.

IMPORTANT: Even if conflicts of interest do not actually lead to un-ethical behavior, just the appearance of or possibility of unethical behavior is enough to undermine public trust and employee confidence in the company's ethical compass.

9

SOX OBLIGATIONS AND PROTECTIONS

ANTIDISCRIMINATION AND DISCLOSURES
OF PERSONAL RELATIONSHIPS

Your company will no doubt take the opportunity to document and train all employees about its expectations regarding workplace behavior in terms of harassment and discrimination. SOX is, after all, a statement and confirmation about workplace ethics and behavior. Reminding everyone of their right to enjoy—and ensure—a workplace that is free from inappropriate workplace behavior consequently lies right at the heart of SOX's ethics message.

First, understand that if you are a supervisor and develop a personal romantic relationship with a subordinate, then that romantic relationship must be disclosed. That's fairly logical: if you have the ability to impact a subordinate's performance review or merit increase, and you suddenly fall out of love, any negative work-related criticism could be viewed as retaliation. Likewise, the prior relationship could be considered inappropriate and possibly constitute sexual harassment. What would be a typical company response to disclosing a romantic relationship with a subordinate? Transferring the subordinate to another unit or supervisor so that there is no immediate threat of retaliation or improper favoritism may provide a simple and fair solution. The key lies in disclosing the new relationship right away before a perception of retaliation or harassment ever has a chance of rearing its ugly head.

Keep in mind that organizations expect you to proactively escalate matters in the spirit of "disclosure and review," meaning that together you will find a solution. Fewer organizations these days have nonfraternization policies (sometimes known as dating policies or workplace romance policies), meaning that spouses can't work at the same company or even if a dating relationship begins between coworkers, someone must resign. Note that in some states, such strict policies are illegal, as they punish otherwise private, out-of-work conduct—that is, a consensual romantic relationship. But companies will indeed draw a strong line of distinction when it comes to one spouse, family member, or significant other supervising another and have policies in place that restrict managers and supervisors from dating subordinates. For those reasons, family members are typically assigned to different supervisors, different shifts, or different departments or work groups—again, the standard being to avoid any *perception* of favoritism or conflict of interest.

Second, remember that harassment can take place on duty or off, in the office or on the road. Therefore, you should expect coworkers to treat you with the same respect off-site as in the office. Likewise, you're under no obligation to put up with inappropriate comments or off-color jokes, physical contact (think back rubs), or nonverbal conduct such as leering or staring. Any such incidents should be reportable to a flexible reporting chain within your organization, including your supervisor, department head, human resources, labor relations, or other company compliance officers (typically corporate counsel).

Be aware, however, that absolute confidentiality cannot be guaranteed if you make a claim that requires an investigation (and almost all claims do). Of course, all reports should be treated as confidential to the extent appropriate. But human resources or the individual conducting the investigation will very likely be obligated to expand that investigation on a "need to know" basis and ultimately bring your complaint to the individual charged. Such confrontation is never easy, but again, your company's anti-discrimination policies and practices, along with federal and/or state law, provide appropriate protections from retaliation when the complaint of harassment is made in good faith.

Finally, remember that disclosing the family relationships of new hires is also typically required under most organizations' codes of conduct. While it's not unlawful for three or even four generations of the same family to work at the same organization, it's critical that these relationships are disclosed at the time of hire. After all, perceptions of unfairness and favoritism are not uncommon when one or more family members side with each other against coworkers. Again, employees should follow the guideline and corporate expectation of disclosure and review, right from the start. The new hire should disclose on the employment application any other family members working at the facility, and existing employees should disclose that family members are about to join the organization—either by updating their "Conflict of Interest Questionnaire" or via email to their supervisors. Establish this expectation going forward to avoid unnecessary drama or potential conflict on your team.

SOX OBLIGATIONS AND PROTECTIONS

COMPANY PROPERTY, WHISTLEBLOWER PROTECTION, SAFETY, PRIVACY, AND INTELLECTUAL PROPERTY

A critical obligation that you have to your company lies in your use of company property. From an employment law perspective, the law generally requires that employers have a written policy stating that workers do not have a reasonable expectation of privacy while using the company email server, company-issued computers, telephones, and tablets. As such, your email and voicemail as well as desks and lockers are company property. Expect your company to reiterate this point during SOX training. Company systems are for company use. Don't let your staff members falsely assume otherwise.

Oh, and don't forget the more-common-than-we'd-like-to-believe problem about pornography on the internet. Just because you close your door and draw your shade doesn't mean that you couldn't be terminated even for a first offense of viewing pornography in the workplace. Many employees seem to forget that their internet visits are traceable. What do you do, however, if you accidentally connect to a website that contains inappropriate information like pornography? Disconnect the second you realize that you shouldn't be there. Then immediately call human resources or IT, explain the situation, and forward them the email link that you accidentally opened in order to make a record of the unintended site visit.

Additional areas covered under an organization's code of conduct include:

WHISTLEBLOWER PROTECTIONS

Section 806 of the act prohibits retaliation against any employees of a publicly traded company who make good faith complaints or disclose illegal activities by their employers that could ultimately constitute material fraud against shareholders. Here again, SOX has teeth: employers will be subject to fines and up to ten years in prison for retaliating against informants.

For that reason, you can expect your company's code of conduct to emphasize the importance of a flexible reporting chain when lodging a complaint. The whole thrust of SOX centers on disclosure and review. A company can fix only the problems it is made aware of, and if employees fear going to their immediate supervisors, they must be given the chance to speak with other senior leaders in the company. That's why many publicly traded companies provide their worldwide employees with phone numbers and email addresses of senior corporate leaders and even audit committee board members. Employees may contact the board directly, either confidentially or by disclosing their names. Either way, employees have direct and immediate access right to the top of the corporation.

SAFETY

Generally speaking, codes of ethics and conduct should ensure full and complete compliance with all potentially applicable regulations, including SOX, Securities and Exchange Commission rules,

NYSE/NASDAQ rules, and other laws and regulations, including occupational safety and health (OSHA). Therefore, while not necessarily codified under the Sarbanes-Oxley Act, businesses have a legal and moral obligation to provide safe work environments for their employees. Yet stories abound of organizations that cut corners and budgets and that could have prevented worker injuries and deaths—think British Petroleum's Deepwater Horizon oil rig in the Gulf of Mexico and so many other high-profile cases in which workplaces literally turned into death traps. As such, you can expect your employer to publish strict guidelines on employee safety standards, both to prevent worker injuries and costly lawsuits that result. All employees are expected to act in a manner that avoids potential health and safety hazards, and they are likewise required to notify their supervisors of any actual or unsafe working conditions or practices observed. Further, if workers witness or are involved in an accident or occurrence that has caused or may lead to injury or damaged property, they must disclose this to management, typically in the form of a report that creates a record of the hazard for senior management's review and intervention.

PRIVACY

Protecting workers' privacy is a hot legal and ethical issue these days. In fact, you could argue that privacy and the protection of personal information is one of the hottest topics of the early twenty-first century. High-profile cases of stolen or compromised computer data add significantly to concerns about privacy and personal safety. Further, from an ethics standpoint, technology allows employers to gain unprecedented knowledge about employee or job applicant behavior. For example, ground zero of where employee privacy meets employment law can be found in the Genetic

Information Nondiscrimination Act, or GINA, which protects Americans from discrimination based on their genetic information in both health insurance and employment. The rise in remote work can create unique challenges in which companies and managers have greater access to the "insides" of an employee's home. Likewise, additional privacy laws surrounding the prehiring process, including "ban-the-box" legislation and the Fair Credit Report Act's focus on how consumer credit bureaus can collect, assess, use, and share the data they collect, are likewise contentious topics from time to time. The very depth and breadth of data mined can be mind boggling, and employers have an obligation to ensure that it isn't misused, either through carelessness or malicious intent.

Identity theft is a typical result when virtual data thieves access personnel or payroll records to open fraudulent credit accounts. As such, organizations have a greater legal and moral responsibility to protect the employee data they steward. Under the Fair and Accurate Credit Transaction Act (FACTA), employers can be held responsible for unauthorized use of employees' personal information. FACTA permits both federal and state governments to levy fines against businesses that are negligent in protecting employee data. In fact, several states have enacted laws barring employers from using workers' full Social Security numbers as identifiers on any records, including timecards, insurance cards, and paycheck stubs.

INTELLECTUAL PROPERTY

The use of company confidential business information for personal gain or advantage is prohibited. In the course of work, employees may learn of trade secrets and commercially or financially sensitive information. In addition, an individual may create or develop systems, procedures, or processes that constitute confidential information and remain the property of the employer. Confidential information may not be used or disclosed to any outside party without prior written authorization from senior management and in compliance with departmental policies.

Confidential business information may include business plans or projections, expansion or curtailment of operations, a merger or acquisition proposal or agreement, customer lists, vendor or supplier lists, proprietary computer software, information on clients, pending litigation, unusual or sensitive management developments or situations, or purchases or sales of substantial assets. Instead, confidential company or business information should be shared with others only when required in the normal course of business (that is, when they have a legitimate need to know the information in the scope of their duties). Confidentiality, noncompete, and nondisclosure agreements are all tools in the trade of protecting intellectual property.

On the flip side, employees must not disclose to their company information from another company learned under circumstances in which the other company had a reasonable expectation that the information would be kept confidential. In other words, confidential information is not a matter of show and tell: your organization neither wants its confidential information shared, nor does it want confidential information from any other company coming to their attention. Ditto for speaking with the media: if you're not appointed by your organization to speak with the media, then you have no business sharing any information with the media, confidentially or otherwise. In other words, when it comes to speaking with the media, if you don't know who's responsible for that, it's not you.

11

WHISTLEBLOWERS
VERSUS CHARACTER ASSASSINS
DEALING WITH ANONYMOUS AND
MEAN-SPIRITED COMPLAINTS

Wait a minute, though. While it's true that all employees should
be protected from retaliation for blowing the whistle on an
unlawful activity or their boss's inappropriate conduct that may
violate antidiscrimination policies, those claims have to be lodged
in good faith. Most companies grant their employees the discretion to escalate matters anonymously, and well they should:
whether the company is publicly traded or privately held, organizations want employees to have immediate and direct access to the
board of directors or heads of the organization in most instances.
After all, if the company isn't aware of a problem because an employee doesn't know how to escalate a claim and bring it to senior
management's attention, then the C-level (that is, CEOs, CFOs,
and COOs) won't learn of a problem until it's potentially too late.
That's why many privately held companies ascribe to the code of
conduct mantra, even though they're not legally required to. It just
makes good business sense.

There can be a downside to such openness and transparency,
however. Allowing employees free rein to complain anonymously
about managers and supervisors may inadvertently open up a

Pandora's box of unfounded allegations that allows workers to engage in character attacks with apparent impunity. Likewise, because workers have become savvy to the whistleblower protections contained in many companies' written policies, many have figured out that engaging in the proverbial *preemptive strike*—"I'll complain about my boss's *conduct* before she has a chance to complain about my job *performance*"—could provide them with a cloak of protection in the form of a retaliation charge against the company should the organization later come back and attempt to terminate, demote, or otherwise take some form of adverse action against them after filing a complaint.

So, how do you, as a responsible corporate leader, handle it when you suspect that the nameless voice behind an anonymous complaint is actually engaging in character assassination against you, the targeted supervisor? How do you appropriately respond to an unknown member of your team who may appear to be spouting unfounded rumors and gossiping freely, sending the company on one wild goose chase after another? Finding that delicate balance between the individual privacy rights of complainants and what could appear to be mean-spirited slander toward the alleged wrongdoer (often the supervisor) places every department head and human resources executive in an ethical quandary, besides placing the company in a compromising legal position. Attacking workplace problems like this directly and appropriately poses exceptional challenges to even the strongest companies and most confident leaders alike, so an approach that combines both legal guidance and common sense will work best. When allegations are raised against you, you can expect HR, corporate counsel, or an outside investigator to conduct a fact-specific and detailed investigation—just be sure to remove yourself from the process in order to avoid any potential perception of influencing the investigation's results.

For instance, a workplace allegation that someone is engaging in timecard fraud may be fairly simple to investigate and verify. But what about an anonymous letter that alleges that Supervisor X is sleeping with a subordinate? And what if that anonymous complaint appears in the ombudsman's mailbox at the same time that the supervisor's wife receives an anonymous text message alleging that her husband is sleeping with that same subordinate? That's when things can get ugly and personal, and the targeted supervisor will often feel he's being attacked at work at the same time that he's attempting desperately to repair his relationship with his wife on the home front. It's a classic situation of the gun being pointed at the employer's head from two different directions—the anonymous complainant who's arguing discrimination, harassment, and potential retaliation on the one hand with the supervisor threatening a defamation lawsuit on the other.

To resolve these types of character assassination attempts, HR will typically first ask the anonymous complainant (who typically makes the company aware of the problem via email from a made-up address) to make him- or herself known so that the organization can work on finding a solution together. If that doesn't work, HR often follows up by asking who should be interviewed to verify the allegations. At the initial stage of the investigation, the anonymous complainant is clearly calling the shots, but HR's attempt to involve the person in the investigation process is both the right thing to do and the most legally practical solution.

What happens next depends on your initial findings. If HR can identify little if any corroborating evidence to substantiate the initial anonymous complaint, it might make most sense for HR to conclude the investigation quietly. HR will simply notify the complainant that it has completed an initial investigation and can't find merit to the claim, so after checking with legal, HR is opting to conclude the investigation with a "no findings call." The investigation will simply be closed and nothing further will be said—unless the individual opts to emerge from the shadows and provide HR with additional information.

On the other hand, HR or senior leadership may wish to take a different route. As is often the case in these types of investigations, the claims raised can be exaggerated, taken out of context, or appear to assign some form of ill intent to the supervisor's actions where none was intended. When a claim appears to lack any form of merit, HR may advise an operational leader not to just close out the investigation and sweep it under the rug; instead, HR may want to partner with you to address the matter openly with your team or department to help "heal the wound."

If that's the case, HR (or your immediate supervisor) might consider addressing the matter as follows: First, check with in-house or outside counsel to ensure that you're getting appropriate legal advice to help you line up your arguments for addressing the team. Second, ensure that your senior leadership team agrees that this approach of addressing the matter openly with the rest of the team in HR's presence makes sense. The HR investigator or your superior—with you present—could then set the stage for a group "investigational wrap-up" meeting as follows:

> HR: While I'm not planning on going into detail about the investigation that we've been conducting for the past two days, I want you all to know that we've fulfilled our commitment as a responsible employer to conduct a thorough investigation in a timely manner and reach a reasonable conclusion.
>
> But I'm not comfortable just closing out this investigation without addressing the elephant in the room. We don't know who filed the original allegation, and that's fine. But I want to remind you all

that real damage can be done to someone's career and personal life when anonymous complaints are made behind the scenes with apparent impunity.

Your Superior / Department Head: I'm disappointed in how this matter was escalated: the allegations appear to have been grossly exaggerated, the witnesses couldn't support the allegations, and this felt like a very personal attack against John. In addition, we've invited the anonymous complainant multiple times to work with me and with HR to get to the bottom of this, but to no avail: the anonymous complainant failed to come forward. That being said, what was said about John was unjustified and mean spirited, which is why I invited John to this meeting. John, I want to apologize to you on behalf of the team for what occurred here. I think you deserve to hear that publicly, and I'm very sorry.

As for the rest of the team, if you have legitimate issues or concerns, feel free to raise them openly by meeting with me or file your complaints anonymously—but please remember that there are real people whose careers may be placed at risk, and I expect you all to act in a more responsible manner in the future. This investigation is officially concluded. But I have higher expectations of you as a team than you've displayed here. We're better than this. Anyone who could lodge unfounded complaints about one member of our team could raise them against any of us. I expect more of you, and you should expect more of yourselves. I hope you all take the time to consider how this might have felt to John, to members of his family, and to other members of the team. Let's all move forward with a higher level of awareness and appreciation for the company, for the jobs we have, and for those we work with. And let's make sure we do a much better job of assuming good intentions and having one another's backs.

With this public apology to the wronged supervisor in place, along with a resetting of group expectations, you stand the greatest chance of healing the wound while enforcing your company's escalation policy and whistleblower protections. Addressing the matter openly and honestly can provide a healing touch that will go a long way in preventing future whimsical attacks from behind an anonymous curtain while allowing your team to rebuild fractured relationships and reinstitute a healthy sense of camaraderie. And don't forget the importance of peer awareness: while management may not know who filed the anonymous complaint, members of the team likely do. Addressing the matter openly like this may not fix the problem from the top down but may go a long way in fixing it "from the sides in." Peer influence can be a useful tool in influencing group behavior. Used properly in circumstances where management may appear to be the victim, it can become an optimal tool in influencing errant workers' behaviors.

12

INTERNAL WORKPLACE INVESTIGATIONS
YOUR FIRST LINE OF DEFENSE

Conducting workplace investigations is as much an art as it is a science, and this exercise should generally be left to human resources or some other neutral third party, especially if the claim is against you, the manager. On the other hand, it's important that you understand the basics of workplace investigations in case you need to partner with HR, an external consultant, or an attorney (to preserve privilege, among other reasons) who may be looking into allegations that potentially involve members of your team. One thing is for sure, though—it's critical that all members of management involved are clearly operating under the same assumptions and conducting their fact-finding missions consistently.

While no book on a topic this broad can replace sound legal advice based on fact-specific situations that may come your way case-by-case as an employer, it's critical to understand the basics of workplace investigations because so many companies trip themselves up and step on land mines by not following their own internal rules or basic guidelines for fairness and due process. Your goals in conducting workplace investigations should be threefold:

■ Ensure fairness, consistency, and high morale on the one hand, while protecting your company legally on the other.

■ Know when to recuse yourself from an investigation due to a potential conflict of interest or the possibility of garnering a retaliation claim by simply participating in the process.

■ Communicate appropriately both verbally and in writing when it comes to documenting your findings and reaching a timely and reasonable conclusion.

To the first point above, understand that workplace investigations, by their very nature, create tremendous anxiety and angst among affected team members. As a result, investigations should be completed as quickly as possible and shouldn't linger on or remain open ended. In other words, rip the bandage off all at once, if at all possible. In terms of your formal legal obligation as an employer, here is what courts expect of employers involved in such activities:

> The employer is obligated to conduct a timely investigation and to reach a reasonable conclusion.

That's it! You're not expected to have a magic wand that looks into the hearts and souls of your employees. Courts realize that investigations are limited by their very nature and as a result have deemed that legal standards such as "guilty beyond reasonable doubt" or "guilty by a preponderance of the evidence" are not thresholds that apply to workplace investigations. You simply have to act reasonably, responsibly, and in a timely manner to reach a reasonable conclusion. That being said, you have to use common sense: listen to both sides of a story before taking action, investigate any witnesses or review documents that can substantiate someone's claim, and ensure that the written record that justifies a particular course of action (especially termination) is thorough, well documented, and well thought through. And, of course, take prompt and remedial action to put an end to a problem that you learn about as a result of a good faith complaint.

To the second point above, there will be times when you're not allowed to participate in an investigation in any way simply because of the nature of your role within the organization (for example, as an immediate supervisor, department head, or division head). Simply put, if someone on your team could accuse you of potential retaliation for simply participating in an investigation, you have to respectfully decline to be involved. In fact, you might consider recommending that you work from home on the day the investigation takes place so that no one can accuse you of somehow influencing the outcome of the investigation by simply being on company premises.

There's another critical consideration, however. Business conduct statements often confirm that "Employees and supervisors may not conduct their own investigation." Heed those words carefully: trying to unduly influence an investigation can have far more damaging results than the original underlying cause of the investigation itself!

That's because any perception of attempting to influence or affect what should be an objective and dispassionate workplace investigation is a significant breach of workplace conduct that could result in immediate dismissal. Companies can't mess around with bending ethical rules at the time of an investigation, and propriety may dictate that anyone trying to unduly influence the outcome of an investigation be terminated because of the ethical perception problem created. After all, when it comes to matters of ethics in the workplace, the issue drives the outcome: no matter how much tenure you have, how popular you are, or how successful you might be, a significant ethical breach may leave a company with no choice but to terminate—even for a first offense. In short, you may be messing with fire here, so be very cautious so as not to get burned.

Likewise, don't ever make statements to your staff members about "not going to HR" or "keeping everything that goes on within our department *within the family*." Too many managers try to control their teams by throwing out veiled or even direct threats about employees escalating issues outside the group. This is a career land mine for one simple reason: you'll have created a public record that all employees on your team can attest to regarding the fact that you somehow threatened them—either directly or by employing some type of veiled threat—that they'd be disciplined, terminated, or otherwise retaliated against for escalating matters beyond your immediate control. Again, that fact alone could warrant significant corrective action or even termination against you—regardless of the severity of the issue at hand.

And remember that angry employees have long memories: if someone on your team suspects that you may be looking to discipline or terminate them six months or a year later, that employee— likely a very sophisticated consumer—may report to human resources that they feel intimidated working for you and that you're creating a hostile work environment. How? "My boss threatened us last spring by telling us if anyone was thinking of going to HR to lodge a complaint, he'd find out who they were and find a way to terminate them." And HR, of course, can very easily determine that this threat was true: after all, the manager warned the entire team all at the same time! So there you have it—fifteen employees and fifteen witnesses who can substantiate this aggrieved worker's complaint to HR. And my, oh my . . . doesn't that muddy up the waters when you may otherwise have legitimate performance reasons to discipline or terminate this individual?

Instead, encourage the employees on your team to escalate matters to your boss, to the department or division head, to human resources, or even to the company's in-house counsel if they feel that's warranted. Explain that you would generally appreciate a heads-up of a complaint escalating beyond your department to some other member of the company's leadership team, but that's optional. What's more important is that everyone on your team understands and feels comfortable with escalating a matter outside of your group at any time if they feel it is warranted. That's the public record you want to have in place in terms of formally addressing your team regarding workplace complaints or other concerns. It's open, reasonable, and fair. Likewise, it builds trust and creates a healthy culture of transparency. But at its core, it creates a record—witnessed by your staff members—attesting to your willingness to allow others to escalate matters beyond your immediate group if they feel that's necessary. And that protects you. Simply put, establishing your expectations publicly this way will indeed protect you one day if a workplace investigation ever materializes where you're accused of some type of wrongdoing.

To the third point above, remember that you're not in this alone. When a workplace investigation rears its head—whether you're accused or you're involved in the fact-finding mission—remember that you cannot overcommunicate to HR, the investigator, or your in-house counsel. Play-by-play action is expected and is the norm: remember that the timeliness of your investigation is one of the expectations that a court will have of you both as the supervisor and as the employer. So your rule is to "communicate, communicate, communicate" in terms of your findings, new leads, additional witnesses, or potential changes in course that you learn of. I can't overemphasize how important timely communication is during an investigation. Besides, you're not a professional investigator—this is only one of a hundred things you're asked to do at any given time—so depend on the professionals and stay close to them both to protect yourself and the company.

Finally, never rush to judgment at the finish line. If you need additional time to look into particular matters, simply place the accused employee on a paid, investigatory leave. This buys you additional time to confirm facts, research documents, and interview witnesses. Too many companies rush to the firing stage, only to learn in the litigation arena that they didn't do their homework, hadn't interviewed the witnesses, or hadn't reviewed the documents recommended by the complainant (that is, the accused ex-employee who's now bringing suit against your company for wrongful termination). Slow down at the finish line before you reach a final conclusion and make sure all involved parties (operations, legal, and HR) agree with the final decision. This way, if a lawsuit does eventually come your way, there will be no surprises, and everyone will be on the same page in terms of defending it.

POLICIES (THE LETTER OF THE LAW), CODES OF CONDUCT (THE SPIRIT OF THE LAW), AND PAST PRACTICES

Have you ever wondered why companies have so many documents addressing employment in the workplace? Policy and procedure manuals, employee handbooks, business conduct statements, mission, vision, and value declarations, and the like all serve different purposes, and it's important that you understand their function. What's more important, however, is to understand that *practice trumps policy*. In other words, what your company actually does with your policies is more significant in a court of law than what a handbook or policy and procedure manual says you're *supposed* to do. Let's look at past practices first.

As a rule, don't get too lost in what your handbook or policy and procedure manual tells you that you may do in specific instances. Generally speaking, you have to look at the "totality of events" involved in any given situation and at your organization's past practices. (You'll generally get that information when escalating the matter to HR or your organization's legal counsel.) For example, if a supervisor complains to you that a team member told him to "f-off," your first reaction might be to terminate that individual—no questions asked. But what if the manager used that very same terminology on the employee first? Would you still argue that the subordinate should be fired? Or should they both be fired? And what if everyone on the team uses that expression as a term for kidding around with one another: Is it justifiable to take one instance in isolation and out of context and then terminate someone for gross insubordination?

The lesson is that you've got to look to how your company has handled similar situations in the past. Looking at any one event in isolation—no matter how egregious—could show that you didn't do your homework before reaching a conclusion about the case. Remember that there are two sides to every story, and acting on only one side may leave your company vulnerable and exposed when it comes time to explain the rationale behind your final decision to terminate in light of the incomplete investigation that your organization conducted (or so reasons the plaintiff's attorney). Again, bear in mind that the policy exists as a guideline, but it's only as valuable as how consistently it's enforced across the board.

Workplace policies and procedures, in comparison, are important because they prescribe how to go about dealing with particular employee challenges in the office or on the shop floor: antidiscrimination, overtime, substance abuse, and other policies are designed to walk you through the steps necessary to successfully manage problems that come up. As a rule of thumb, though, whenever you sense yourself reaching for the employee handbook or departmental policy and procedure manual, make a quick call to HR, in-house legal counsel, or another similar group to see how the company has handled similar situations in the past. First, you'll gain a quick understanding that you're not alone in experiencing this type of problem and that HR has probably seen and dealt with similar situations in the past. Second, you'll get a quick overview of how your company's past practices have played themselves out so that you're not basing your decision exclusively on what the "good book" says you're supposed to do. Third, remember that most companies practice the "rules are meant to be broken" adage from time to time under extenuating circumstances, so a quick call to HR is in your and the company's best interests to see how closely your organization has historically followed that particular policy or standard operating procedure.

If policies outline the letter of the law as your company defines them, then codes of conduct, otherwise known as corporate ethics statements, address the spirit of the law. Corporate ethics statements are not intended for line-by-line interpretation; instead, they're designed to cast a much broader net that speaks to worker ethics, morals, and appropriate workplace conduct. Let's look at an example. A biopharmaceutical company works with blood-related products, with blood samples being drawn from facilities around the country. One particular blood bank facility is run by a wife and husband team, in which the wife is the general manager (GM), and the husband is the head of quality. (The head of quality reports to the GM.) The GM was arrested for illegal drug possession. Did the head of quality (the husband) have an obligation to report the GM's (his wife's) arrest to the corporate headquarters?

The HR head argued yes—the head of quality had an affirmative obligation to disclose his wife's arrest: she's the GM of the facility, she would be missing work for a specific period of time, and she was arrested for unlawful drug possession, which has direct bearing on a biopharmaceutical company that works with blood products and creates medicines derived from the blood products collected. Interestingly enough, the corporate head of quality argued the opposite: a husband has no obligation to disclose his wife's arrest, regardless of the reason for the arrest. To quote the head of quality: "Show me in the employee handbook or the policy and procedure manual where it states that one spouse has to turn in another spouse and potentially cause that person to lose his or her job."

The HR executive's response: "You're looking at the wrong book. It's not the policy and procedures manual or the employee handbook that governs in cases like this; it's the code of conduct. The reason we discourage direct supervision of one spouse by another—even if they've been working together like this for decades—is to avoid situations like this in which the husband's obligation to his wife conflicts with the head of quality's obligation to the organization. In this case, reporting his wife's arrest to corporate was his affirmative obligation to the company, which he failed to escalate. It's the spirit of the law that was violated here, not any specific letter of the law. The head of quality's obligation to the company takes precedence over his obligation to his wife in this corporate setting, and his decision displays a lack of judgment on his part that seriously affects his credibility in the role. My recommendation is to terminate so that we don't inadvertently create a precedent for similar future occurrences." The organization's legal counsel agreed, and the termination of the head of quality was sustained.

This is a prime example of why companies shouldn't have married couples reporting to one another, especially when they work at an independent facility that has no local oversight.

The point to keep in mind is that, unlike with policies, ethics statements cast a much wider net in terms of capturing employee improprieties. The ends never justify the means. The old excuse "Well, I didn't read that in the handbook" goes out the window in an environment where workers, and especially leaders, are held to much higher behavioral standards. Employees are likewise obligated to participate in good faith corporate investigations: they do not have the right to play the part of the deaf, mute, and blind monkey that hears, says, and sees nothing. Similarly, the typical code of conduct stipulates that managers have an obligation to be aware of their surroundings and have an affirmative obligation to escalate and disclose perceived incidents of harassment, retaliation, or conflicts of interest—even if those activities occur in someone else's department. Corporate leaders no longer have the discretion to say, "I don't want to get involved." If they knew, or should have known, what's been going on and failed to disclose it appropriately, they could be individually disciplined or terminated for their lack of discretion and failure to abide by the company's code of conduct.

DELIBERATE IGNORANCE (AKA "WILLFUL BLINDNESS THEORY")

"Knowing" means not only having actual knowledge but also acting with deliberate ignorance or reckless disregard for the truth or falsity of the information. Someone acts with deliberate ignorance by pretending not to see something. Deliberate ignorance also includes acting as if "it's someone else's problem" and is treated as a state of mind equally culpable as actual knowledge.

"Acting with reckless disregard" means that you choose not to investigate a potential problem. The purpose of the willful blindness theory is to impose criminal liability on leaders who recognize the likelihood of wrongdoing but nevertheless consciously refuse to take basic investigatory steps to address and mitigate the situation.

SOX certainly caught corporate America's attention. Any time a new law threatens criminal sanctions against a company's CEO and CFO, you can expect that law to garner lots of attention in the press as well as in company operations. SOX is a broad law that impacts ethical business issues ranging from antitrust and insider information matters to political and charitable contributions and international antiboycott laws. Its most significant contribution will no doubt lie in its emphasis on financial compliance and internal controls.

Its essence focuses on human behavior and ethics, and companies that undergo "best practices SOX training" will reemphasize the importance of maintaining a work environment that upholds the highest standards of business ethics and workplace behavior. Your rights and responsibilities are now more clearly outlined and defined than ever before, and for that you can be grateful, both as an employee and an investor.

PART 3

AVOIDING LITIGATION LAND MINES

14

HE'S EMPLOYED AT WILL

CAN'T WE JUST FIRE HIM?

Have you ever wondered, "Why can't we just fire employees if they're employed at will?" or "Don't we have total discretion to terminate at whim [that is, without cause] for substandard job performance or inappropriate workplace conduct?" You'll understand your rights and limitations a lot better once you have a firmer grasp of employment law history. At the time of our nation's founding in the eighteenth century, US employment law borrowed much of what existed in England at the time, where "termination for just cause only" was the standard. In fact, the Fourteenth Amendment to our constitution later guaranteed, among other rights, workplace due process, based on the fact that the right to work was so fundamental to US citizens that it shouldn't be taken away arbitrarily or without due process of law. In essence, workers had a property right to their jobs, and companies were not at liberty to terminate without just cause or good reason.

That all changed in the 1930s at the time of the Great Depression. The very existence of capitalism appeared to be under threat, and Congress pulled out all the stops to ensure that companies could stay in business. The employment-at-will relationship was born, and the employment property right shifted to companies, which suddenly retained full discretion to terminate at whim.

After World War II, unions gained a stronghold in corporate America. But it wasn't for the reasons most people expect. When polled, most respondents believe that the ability to collectively bargain for better wages and benefits drove union growth from the late 1940s through the 1950s. In reality, it was the unions' promise of job security in the form of workplace due process that sent membership ranks through the roof. The promise went, if your company becomes unionized, you won't be employed at will. The company will have to follow a termination-for-just-cause-only standard, meaning that you can't be terminated at whim and must generally be informed in writing if your job performance is a problem or your position is at risk. Workers flocked to unions as a result, with union membership reaching its peak in the 1950s when roughly 35 percent of the US workforce fell under some form of a collective bargaining agreement. Today, that percentage is closer to 12 percent of the workforce (with the majority in public-sector organizations).

One key reason for the decline in union membership is the advent of tort law. In the 1980 case *Tameny v. Arco Oil,* then California Supreme Court justice Rose Byrd ruled that a fifteen-year employee who refused to engage in price fixing on the employer's behalf couldn't be fired under the employment-at-will umbrella. The public-policy exception was born, and exceptions to the employment-at-will practices made it much more difficult for companies to terminate using the employment-at-will affirmative defense. Specifically, four major categories of exceptions to employment-at-will included:

■ Public-policy exceptions (for example, as in the *Tameny* case, in which whistleblowing or otherwise engaging in protected,

concerted activities eliminated a company's ability to
terminate at whim under the employment-at-will affirmative
defense)

- Statutory exceptions (that is, protected classes, like those
outlined in Title VII of the Civil Rights Act of 1964, which
prohibits discrimination on the basis of sex, race, color,
religion, or national origin)
- Employment contracts (including collective bargaining
agreements)
- Implied contract exceptions/implied covenants of good faith
and fair dealing (especially pertaining to potential promises
made in employee handbooks)

Today, plaintiffs' attorneys, rather than unions, serve primarily as
the mechanism to remedy employer malfeasance in the workplace.
The concept of workplace due process is still at issue when it comes
to litigating employment claims. What's key, however, is that employers understand how the dual standards of employment-at-will
versus termination for just cause only are used in the courtroom.

The employment-at-will affirmative defense is applied at the hearing stage with the goal of gaining an immediate dismissal of the case
in the form of a summary judgment. The company will argue that
the former employee was employed at will and that the company
did nothing to repeal the employment-at-will relationship. Therefore, the company's defense attorney will request that the court dis-
miss the case by relying on the employment-at-will relationship that
the company had established with its ex-worker. If the judge grants
a summary judgment based on the employment-at-will affirmative
defense, the case ends at the hearing stage, plain and simple.

Unfortunately for most corporate defense attorneys, 90 percent
of claims don't get dismissed at the summary judgment hearing

stage—they continue on to the next stage in the litigation process: the trial. Once the case is escalated to trial, there's almost no such thing as the employment-at-will affirmative defense any longer. At the trial stage, the only standard that likely will be considered is termination for just cause only. So, once a case makes it to trial, our legal system reverts back to the termination-for-just-cause-only standard established in the eighteenth century. And as the saying goes, *if it wasn't written down, it never happened.*

Therefore, practically speaking, companies can't terminate workers solely based on the fact that they're employed at will. Without a crystal ball, the company can't know whether it will win a summary judgment at the hearing stage using the employment-at-will affirmative defense or if the case will proceed to trial. As a result, when it comes to relying on the employment-at-will status of a worker versus documenting progressive discipline to prove that a company had cause to terminate, it's not one or the other—it's both. Every company should attempt to protect the employment-at-will relationship with its workers (for the sake of winning a summary judgment at the hearing stage) but also be prepared to show that it had cause to terminate should the case escalate to the trial stage. That cause to terminate is typically found in the form of documented progressive disciplinary warnings and failed annual performance reviews—and you'll sure be glad you have them if a claim escalates to trial.

P.S. The next time someone asks, "Can't we just fire them since they're hired at will?" you can respond by saying, "No way. Employment-at-will only exists in the courtroom, not in the workplace. We have only a 10 percent chance of prevailing at the hearing stage and winning a summary judgment, and those odds are way too risky for me. Let's make sure our documentation is in order so we'll be sure we can win at trial." They'll be so impressed!

15

THE ABSOLUTE RULE OF "DOCUMENT, DOCUMENT, DOCUMENT" AND ITS SIGNIFICANT LIMITATIONS

The importance of documenting substandard job performance and inappropriate workplace conduct is of critical importance in defending cases at trial. But even more significant, it's fair for your employees. Indicating areas where improvement is needed creates an ethical workplace where employees feel valued and where turnarounds based on leadership interventions like progressive discipline, coupled with training, provide all workers with an equal opportunity to improve otherwise poor performance records. In fact, your organization's responsibility as a good corporate citizen is to be able to demonstrate and prove its affirmative efforts in rehabilitating its workers. That's the standard, after all, that will be explained to juries who will be responsible for determining if your organization acted in good faith relative to an ex-employee's termination.

But two common errors occur in the documentation process itself: employers often issue corrective action inappropriately and later contradict the written records they create when drafting annual performance reviews. Let's briefly look at both scenarios. In the first instance, organizations issue progressive discipline in the form of documented verbal, written, and final written warnings like they're giving out hotcakes. Issuing progressive discipline is not merely an act of pointing out errors in documented form. It's all about pointing out errors, documenting the negative organizational consequences of the employee's action, resetting expectations, providing training to help employees improve their performance or conduct, offering resources (like an EAP) for the employee to reach out to privately, inviting the employee to rebut the warning, and clearly documenting the outcomes and consequences for failure to demonstrate immediate and sustained improvement. Phew . . . that sounds like a lot! But it's actually fairly reasonable. After all, you're *not* just pointing out failures or shortcomings—you're attempting in writing to provide the employee with the resources, guidance, and tools to improve the situation at hand.

Therefore, if your "written warning" consists of one piece of paper with three to five sentences on it, you're not *really* providing thorough corrective action. It could be difficult to win at trial if you present such scant evidence of your organization's "good faith attempts at proactively rehabilitating the worker." Instead, make sure your documentation is thorough, reasonable, and can tell its own story of how the organization has tried to help. If progressive discipline is truly doing its job, it will point to a written record that can stand on its own, revealing an employee who refused the help offered by a generous and responsible company and who therefore terminated himself.

Scant documentation is a significant problem in many organizations, and it shows itself clearly at the time of trial preparation. But there's something even scarier than that: documentation that never makes its way to the employee in the first place! Many employers follow a "document-document-document" strategy as recommended by many an attorney in annual employment law updates. But here's the catch: if you don't share the documentation with the employee at the time of the problematic occurrence, the documentation itself has little value. As an HR practitioner myself, I've met with supervisors who bring pages and pages of "proof" that the employee has been performing poorly. When I ask them whether they had shared this information with the employee at the time of the incident, however, they sheepishly admit that they did not. My typical response is, "Well, you can take it off my desk, because if it wasn't shared with the employee when it occurred—either as a discussion topic or training tool or in the form of formal corrective action [aka progressive discipline]—it has little value in terms of the record that we're looking at today." In short, we often have to start with the first level of progressive discipline—a documented verbal warning—even though there were enough problems to terminate the individual several times over.

But the story gets worse: despite the myriad problems, documented or not, that the manager has had to face for the past year, "grade inflation" occurs on the annual performance review that negates the progressive discipline that's occurred up to this point in time. In other words, by your own documentation and admission, the former problems—sometimes documented as written warnings or even final written warnings—are steamrollered by an annual review that basically codifies that the individual "met expectations" for the performance year. *Ouch!* Here's the key: when discipline occurs throughout the performance period, be sure to capture it in the annual performance review. Likewise, if the employee received multiple accolades from customers in the form of letters of recommendation, reference them in the annual performance review as well. Annual reviews are meant to capture everything. It's not the case that "I documented the problem back in

October and didn't want to bring it up again at the time of the annual review; it would be like punishing the person twice." That type of logic will land you and your organization in hot water any time you're attempting to justify a termination before an arbitrator or court.

WHAT'S WRONG WITH THIS PICTURE?

August: Verbal Warning
October: Written Warning
December: Final Written Warning
February: Annual Performance Review *"Meets Expectations"*
March: Manager Recommends Termination

You guessed it: the "meets expectations" score in the annual performance review appears to validate the individual's performance contribution over the entire past year—despite the verbal, written, and final written warnings issued. That inconsistency in the written record could lead a plaintiff's attorney to argue that you denied your ex-worker due process because the record was confusing and the individual did not believe her position was in serious jeopardy of being lost. Grade inflation on annual performance reviews represents one of the biggest hurdles that companies face when defending against wrongful termination claims.

Final thought (and I promise I'll stop beating on this topic): if you issue too much progressive discipline, that can also weigh against you in court. Yes, there's such a thing as too much corrective action. Multiple verbal warnings, multiple written warnings, and, yes, even multiple final written warnings can come back to haunt you in the litigation arena. That's especially the case when companies issue multiple "final" written warnings. You can imagine a judge or arbitrator asking, "Why does he have three final written warnings on file? Doesn't final mean *final* to you? How was your ex-employee supposed to know when the 'final' written warning was really real? I think you confused him with all this documentation. It's inconsistent with your own policy. In short, this is a mess. Despite your multiple interventions of progressive discipline, I do not believe that you accorded this individual workplace due process. You arbitrarily terminated him, despite multiple final written warnings, so I'm not going to sustain the termination decision you made and will instead substitute my own remedy for what occurred here." Another *ouch*.

When faced with the odd exception of having multiple final written warnings on file, make the "real" and "final" final written warning stand out from the others by adding language like this: "This is your last chance. You will not be issued any further corrective action or final written warnings for this offense or similar offenses. If you ever again engage in behaviors that can appear to humiliate others, strip them of their dignity, shame them publicly, or otherwise fail to create a friendly and inclusive work environment, you will be immediately discharged for cause." See the logic? It's not so hard when you think about it, but most leaders need to understand this critical aspect of consistent disciplinary documentation better.

16

PROPERLY INVOKING THE ATTORNEY-CLIENT PRIVILEGE IN YOUR EMAIL AND WRITTEN CORRESPONDENCE

Many managers progress through their careers without a thorough understanding of employment defense strategies. While you may hope that you never need them, it's wisest to bring yourself up to speed with certain elements of "Business Legal 101" to protect yourself and your organization from unwanted legal exposure. One such area that's really important to understand—but that's rarely taught in business schools or in-house training workshops—is the attorney-client privilege. True, you may not need to use it very often, but it's definitely worth adding to your vocabulary and your leadership toolbox.

The attorney-client privilege is a way to address communication to your outside or in-house counsel when you need to send a message (such as a letter or email) but don't want it to be potentially discoverable by opposing counsel if a lawsuit were to ensue. For example, during the course of a workplace investigation, you may want to protect certain communications or recommendations from being introduced as evidence in later litigation. The attorney-client privilege, if used properly, should accomplish this task.

The attorney-client privilege may be used when a complaint involves serious concerns (including potential criminal claims), may develop into a lawsuit, or may have the potential to affect a large number of employees (for example, class action status), among other considerations. It is always best to contact your legal department in advance of launching an investigation when you suspect that the gravity of the situation may give rise to significant liability. So be sure to discuss up front whether your in-house counsel or outside defense attorney wants any particular emails or document exchanges protected. Further, if you have any question whether you should be invoking the attorney-client privilege, always err on the side of caution and protect the documentation trail as much as possible. Better yet—pick up the phone and call your attorney before committing anything to writing.

Note that there are no absolute guarantees when it comes to invoking the attorney-client privilege. Just because you mark a document "privileged and confidential" doesn't mean that a plaintiff's attorney won't challenge the privilege and that a court won't overturn it. Therefore, let caution rule the day when it comes to exchanging emails, documents, or other electronic communications that you mark privileged. After all, it could come as quite a surprise if a judge allows the communication to be shared with the other party and made part of the public record, even though you thought you followed the steps below properly. The steps that follow will help increase the chances that a particular communication or series of communications can withstand legal scrutiny and remain privileged, but without a crystal ball, you can't guarantee that the privilege will be sustained because a court has the discretion to disallow the privilege.

That being said, you've got to know how to structure an attorney-client privileged communication to maximize the chances of it not being overturned by a court at some point in the future. To do so, follow these general rules:

Rule 1: Pick up the phone before you commit something questionable to writing. Speak with your in-house counsel or external employment lawyer to determine whether the issue is covered by the attorney-client privilege.

Rule 2: Address the communication to your attorney. This could be your in-house counsel or outside counsel, but for the attorney-client privilege to become effective, it must be addressed to an attorney who is providing legal advice and counsel. The privilege does not protect communications between workers when no attorney is present. In other words, you can't send an email to your nonattorney boss and mark it "privileged and confidential" because without an attorney on the receiving end to provide legal analysis and advice, there's no mechanism to protect the communication from legal discovery.

Rule 3: End the communication by asking your attorney for a legal opinion and analysis. You may be challenged in sustaining the privilege if you simply copy your attorney on your various emails without asking for official legal advice. Instead, to sustain the privilege, a judge will generally want to see that you reached out to your attorney for a legal opinion and recommendation. If successful, your description of the facts and your attorney's recommended course of action will be protected from plaintiffs' attorneys' eyeballs (and from a jury's considerations) should the case proceed to trial.

Rule 4: Label the top of the communication or the subject line of an email: "Privileged and Confidential: Attorney-Client Privileged

Communication." This notice should be prominent and easily viewable as soon as someone receives the communication.

Rule 5: Copy only a limited number of people who have a legitimate need to know the information. Do not copy or share the document with others or the privilege may be lost. After all, if you copy fifteen people on the communication, a court will likely infer that it wasn't all that confidential or proprietary to begin with. So, simply including too many people in the communication could jeopardize the privilege. As a rule, try and limit the audience to either only the attorney or to the attorney plus one other person (for example, your boss).

Rule 6: Do not communicate the information discussed with the attorney to others unless instructed to do so. The nature of attorney-client privileged communications is that they are highly confidential, limited in distribution, and created at a particular point in time on a strict need-to-know basis. Failing to create the document under such criteria could result in the loss of the privilege and the subsequent sharing of the material as part of the plaintiff's attorney's case against your company.

EXAMPLE OF AN ATTORNEY-CLIENT PRIVILEGED DOCUMENT STRUCTURE

Subject Line of Email:
Privileged & Confidential: Attorney-Client Privileged Communication

Heading of Email Body:
Privileged & Confidential: Attorney-Client Privileged Communication

Email Content:

Dear Nina [your attorney's name]:

Based on our discussion just now, I'd like your advice and counsel on the following matter . . . [Details Here]

Please provide your legal analysis and opinion at your earliest convenience. Thanks very much.

—Paul

Again, not all attorney-client communications will be deemed privileged once submitted in court, so always proceed with caution and continue to communicate in writing as if your document may be used as evidence in court at some point and blown up on a large electronic screen and placed in front of a jury. You can't be careful enough when it comes to the possibility of your own communication to your attorney being employed as evidence *against* your own company. When in doubt, pick up the phone and call your attorney before hitting the *send* button. To quote the Benjamin Franklin axiom, an ounce of prevention is worth a pound of cure.

NOT ALL HARASSMENT IS SEXUAL

I know you know this, but it's worth taking a quick walk down the path of preventing nonsexual harassment. Why? Because this is all alive and well in courthouses throughout the nation, so you'll want to be doubly sure that you've got a firm grasp on this critical employment law topic. Proactively addressing conduct that can give rise to a nonsexual-harassment-related discriminatory complaint should be part of your leadership toolbox moving forward in your career. First, some definitions:

DISCRIMINATION

Treating an individual differently based on a protected characteristic or classification.

HARASSMENT

Under Title VII: unwelcome or offensive conduct "which is severe or pervasive and creates a hostile work environment." (Note, however, that states may differ from the federal definition by removing the "severe or pervasive" standard in order to make it easier to file and prove harassment claims.)

Some state legislatures have sought to make it easier not only to bring harassment claims but also to prove them by eliminating or encouraging removal of the "severe or pervasive" standard for hostile work environment claims.

Second, understand that claims are often influenced by community movements and events happening at the time. For example, the #MeToo movement (gender), Black Lives Matter (race), and COVID (retaliation and discrimination) triggered lawsuits in their respective areas because awareness within and among those communities grew exponentially during those time periods. Following is a short list to grab your attention and raise your own awareness about how comments that continuously pepper the workplace can give rise to legal action that may be difficult to defend:

Discriminatory Comments
- Discrimination based on presumption ("I'm not Muslim but you assume that I am")
- Discrimination by association ("You've made ongoing comments about my husband having multiple sclerosis")
- Derogatory comments blaming COVID on certain minority groups or races
- Offensive statements about minority outreach activities in recruitment or about equality movements by specific minority groups

Note: Discrimination from people of the same race is possible.

Age

- Age discrimination in furlough or layoff decisions, pandemic stay-at-home orders, or failure to return older workers to work
- Overall treatment of "high risk" employees (age and pregnancy)
- Replacing older employees with substantially younger employees, even if both groups are over forty (Rule of thumb: if there is greater than a ten-year age gap between the two individuals over forty, most plaintiffs' attorneys will often pursue an age discrimination claim)
- Mandatory retirement programs at a specific age
- Disparate impact analysis for reductions in force (which typically occur when companies select individuals for layoff without conducting peer group analysis of those potentially impacted and reviewing that exercise without the help of outside counsel)

Immigration/Hiring Status

- Immigration/citizenship status: refusal to consider valid paperwork as identified in the I-9 form
- "Green card only" hiring rules for immigrants
- English-only speaking rules, which may be permitted but must (1) be justified by business necessity; (2) narrowly tailored; and (3) made known to employees up front (for example, by tying the need to patient care and safety in hospitals)
- Ancestry or national origin status: Note that "place of origin" can be a country, a former country, or an ethnic group that is not a country (for example, Kurdistan); examples include: calling employees by their Caucasian name rather than their ethnic name; making statements like "Your country needs to be nuked," or other terrorist references

- ■ Refusing to hire someone without an "all-American" look or image
- ■ Disparate impact of criminal background checks on decisions not to hire minority applicants

Religion

- ■ Failure to accommodate work schedules (such as, not working on the Sabbath or past sundown)
- ■ Failure to accommodate dress or grooming practices (for example, hijabs or turbans)
- ■ Applying protections to less commonly known religions where a "sincerely held religious belief" may apply

Note: Overall, religious accommodation and discrimination claims are difficult to defend and very fact specific. (1) Fact-specific analysis, (2) legitimate business need, and (3) whether the requested accommodation places an undue burden on the employer are the key considerations in religious discrimination claims.

Disability/Medical Condition

- ■ Failure to modify someone's job or accommodate work restrictions that allow them to continue working
- ■ Medical or casual marijuana usage (which is generally not a reasonable accommodation under the Americans with Disabilities Act, although the laws are continuously changing in this area)

Note: Whenever it comes to workplace restrictions, modified duty, or other accommodations related to medical disabilities—permanent or temporary—it is always best to engage in "reasonable accommodation" discussions as outlined under the ADA's interactive process guidelines.

I know . . . the list is exhausting and overwhelming. It seems like anyone can sue an employer for any one of a million reasons. Well, yes and no. While it's true that a lawsuit can be filed for as little as $100 at your local county courthouse, plaintiffs' attorneys usually work on *contingency,* meaning that they receive compensation only if they win their case. Therefore, many won't accept a case unless they're reasonably sure they can win it. On the other hand, many often accept questionable cases because they figure that most employers would rather pay a nuisance value settlement rather than pay their own attorneys to defend the case. Either way, it's best to avoid plaintiffs' lawsuits at all costs. Generally speaking, keep the following guidelines in mind:

- When looking at the prospect of taking on a new case, plaintiffs' attorneys must find a link to one of the protected classes afforded under federal law (race, color, religion, sex, national origin, age, disability, genetic information, pregnancy, sexual orientation, and gender identity) and/or the various protections available under state law.
- Documentation in the form of progressive discipline typically acts like garlic in keeping the vampires away. Plaintiffs' attorneys want cases in which there is little if any documentation and he said/she said scenarios that can be misconstrued or otherwise cause confusion (which always works to their and their clients' advantage).
- It's all about the written record. When a written record can stand on its own, plaintiffs' lawyers often pass on it. When the

written record is inconsistent, contradictory, or nonexistent, plaintiffs' attorneys will be much more likely to take on the new case.

The way I've always looked at it is, I don't mind getting sued—that's simply the cost of doing business in corporate America from time to time. But what's critically important to me is that I get sued *on my terms*—not theirs. When the documentation is tight and consistent and when multiple witnesses can attest to how fairly the individual was treated or how difficult it was to get along with the worker, then I'm on solid ground to defend a lawsuit that comes my way. The whole purpose of this book and this book series is to prepare you to conduct all your employee relations matters and people practices in a fair and ethical manner, which enhances your organizational culture and your reputation as a leader while minimizing the downside risk of employment litigation and liability.

18

PERFORMANCE VERSUS CONDUCT
A CRITICAL EMPLOYMENT LAW DISTINCTION

O rganizations typically refer to their "standards of performance and conduct" as a general "catchall" for their policies, procedures, and workplace expectations and guidelines. But there's a tremendous difference between a performance infraction and a conduct violation, and it's critical that you understand how they are treated in the workplace.

Performance infractions typically refer to substandard productivity in the areas of quality, quantity, speed, customer service, and even attendance/tardiness (although many companies split attendance out from the broader "performance" category in their progressive disciplinary action policies). When problems occur in these areas, companies are expected to provide "workplace due process" as outlined in their employee handbooks and policy and procedure manuals. Specifically, a step system of increased consequences gets documented each time an additional infraction occurs, and each progressive step contains some added element indicating the severity of the situation if it isn't remedied immediately. Most companies follow a "three strikes and you're out" progressive discipline paradigm that looks something like this:

Step 1: Documented verbal warning
Step 2: Written warning
Step 3: Final written warning

After that final written warning is issued, a "clean" final incident will typically justify termination of employment. There can be exceptions, of course. A new hire that is thirty days into a new position with her company may be terminated without prior written documentation or may receive one documented warning just to protect the company before being dismissed. (It depends on the company's tolerance for risk: some organizations feel that the one written warning will serve as an insurance policy of sorts to keep plaintiffs' attorneys from suing, because "Did you ever receive documented corrective action before you were terminated?" is still one of the first questions that plaintiffs' attorneys ask when considering whether to take on a new case.) On the other hand, a thirty-year employee may be accorded greater workplace due process because of the years of tenure. As an example, the individual may be given a "performance improvement plan" or "letter of clarification" as incremental, additional steps that document the problems without escalating the formal corrective action chain that leads to termination.

Whatever the case, when it comes to performance and attendance infractions, the general expectation is that the company follows its policies and accords workplace due process in the form of stepped-up corrective action notices so that the worker understands what the problem is, what needs to be done to fix the problem, and what the consequences will be for failure to demonstrate improvement within a reasonable period of time.

Not so with conduct infractions: conduct infractions may lead to immediate dismissal even for a first offense when there is no prior corrective action on record. And even if a company opts not to terminate on a first offense, the organization may arguably proceed straight to a final written warning and stop just shy of termination.

You could probably guess that if an employee engages in theft, then termination would be the result—even for a first-time offense. In conduct-related cases, *the issue drives the outcome,* meaning that the company doesn't have the discretion not to terminate (even if it wanted to). It simply has to terminate for the sake of the record that's being created and in order to avoid creating an unwanted precedent. After all, if you don't terminate Employee A for stealing, how could you justify terminating Employee B at some point in the future without looking like a discriminatory employer? Ditto for embezzlement, fraud, egregious cases of sexual harassment, and the like.

This makes horse sense—if someone stole from the company, they should expect to be fired, so you—the manager—probably wouldn't have too much of a challenge justifying termination for someone on your team who took cash out of the till. But what about someone who demonstrates a total disrespect or contempt for their supervisor or coworkers? What about someone who constantly demonstrates a "bad attitude" and kills workplace camaraderie and departmental morale? Many employees mistakenly assume—as do their supervisors—that as long as their performance is acceptable, the company can't do anything to them to address their poor conduct.

Not so. That's a serious mistaken assumption on the employee's part, and a key blind spot for supervisors who don't realize they have discretion to escalate through the progressive discipline process to address the problem. After all, all employees are responsible for *both* their performance *and* conduct: they don't simply get to focus on one and not the other. Everyone is responsible for performing at an acceptable level *and* ensuring that their coworkers feel welcome and comfortable working with them. In short, they're responsible for creating a friendly and inclusive work environment just as you and other members of your team are.

Therefore, think of the performance-conduct circle as two halves of the same whole (see below): you can't have one without the other, and when an investigation reveals that someone is bullying, confrontational, condescending, or otherwise vexing to their supervisor or teammates, remember that you have the discretion to move straight to a final written warning—even for a first offense, if necessary. Again, supervisors often have a lot more discretion than they think and should never feel like they're being held hostage by good performers who otherwise act like worms in an apple.

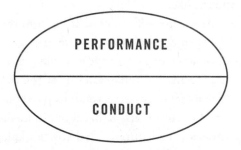

The Performance-Conduct Circle—Employees are responsible for both, so someone who performs well but who demonstrates ongoing behavior and conduct problems is only meeting 50 percent of the job's overall expectations and failing overall.

That being said, if a manager is going to write up an employee for an infraction, absent unique circumstances, the employer must write up other workers for the same infraction. Treating one employee's infraction differently than another is often the basis for a discrimination claim.

19

SAMENESS VERSUS CONSISTENCY
A POTENTIAL ETHICAL QUAGMIRE

Supervisors often make the mistake of assuming that everyone has to be treated exactly the same when, in fact, it's *consistency* they're looking for. There's an expression that says, "If all you have is a hammer, everything starts to look like a nail." Supervisors and managers have more discretion than they think in many circumstances, and simply trying to treat every infraction exactly the same misses the point. Let's look at an example.

Sleeping on the job is a serious infraction in any situation. But does it warrant a first written warning, a final written warning, or outright termination? As with many workplace investigations and employee relations issues, *it depends.* Has the individual caught sleeping done this before? How long was the person asleep? Did the sleeping cause some negative organizational impact that warrants an immediate termination on the one hand or little if any corrective action at all on the other?

Don't look only at the issue of sleeping: it's also about the conditions and circumstances surrounding the act of sleeping that play an important role in rendering an appropriate decision. Here's how companies have ruled in the past:

■ An insurance claims adjustor caught napping at her desk
receives a *first written warning* for sleeping on the job.

■ A charge nurse on the graveyard shift of a hospital's intensive
care unit caught sleeping at the consul is issued a *final written
warning*—even for a first offense—since patients' safety may
be jeopardized.

■ An anesthesiologist who falls asleep during surgery is
terminated outright, seeing that a patient's life may be in
immediate danger.

As you can see, it's not the sleeping per se that drives the outcome: it's the circumstances surrounding the sleeping that must be
considered, and the potential negative organizational consequences
typically drive the employer's decision to act in a certain way.

A company is being consistent when it issues a written warning
for one incident (claims adjuster), a final written warning for another incident (charge nurse), and an immediate dismissal for yet
a third incident (anesthesiologist) under different circumstances.
One size doesn't fit all in the world of workplace investigations and
employee relations, so remember to look at the totality of events
rather than isolated behavioral acts. As always, the best way to determine what an appropriate company response should look like
comes from speaking with human resources, legal, or the department in your organization that deals with employee issues. Just
don't make the call to terminate on your own: there's no reason for
you to assume such an incredible burden, especially when many
states assign *personal legal liability* for what's known as managerial
bad acts.

Yes, you read that correctly: personal liability. Don't inadvertently take on personal liability yourself for issues that occur in the
workplace: they don't pay you enough to shoulder responsibility

that could jeopardize your home or savings. It's a little-known fact that, in many states, managers found guilty of unlawful employment decisions could be personally penalized up to $50,000 for "acting outside the course of scope of their employment." In fact, in the Golden State of California, there's no limit to how much a supervisor can be sued for personally. (Tell me that's not scary!) The best way to insulate yourself from potential charges of personal liability lies in getting the hot potato off your lap and having everything blessed by HR first before taking any type of potentially adverse action (like termination) against one of your employees.

20

ACTING OUTSIDE THE COURSE AND SCOPE OF YOUR EMPLOYMENT

DERAILING AN OTHERWISE BRILLIANT CAREER TRAJECTORY

We can't complete our discussion of workplace investigations without addressing some of the "Big Guns" out there in the workplace: harassment, discrimination, and retaliation complaints that can be so damaging to internal morale and so potentially costly to organizations from a liability standpoint. Here's what the scenario typically looks like: A supervisor fails to disclose to HR or organizational leadership the fact that an employee told him that she (the employee) was feeling harassed. The employee may have asked the supervisor to keep the matter confidential as a personal favor, but in matters regarding (1) harassment or discrimination, (2) potential violence in the workplace, or (3) a conflict of interest with the organization's business interests, supervisors have no discretion: they must affirmatively disclose to the employee that they will be escalating the complaint to HR (or some other party that typically handles employee complaints). In the eyes of the law, once the worker informs a supervisor of the problem, then the *entire company* is deemed to be placed on notice. A supervisor has what's known as an "affirmative obligation to disclose," and any failure to do so will leave the company seriously vulnerable.

There's another, less direct, scenario that's commonly seen when complaints regarding harassment, discrimination, retaliation, or hostile work environment claims go unchecked: a supervisor or member of management simply assumes that if no one makes a formal complaint, then the company has no obligation to act. The "reasonableness" standard holds that if you (for instance, the supervisor or superior) either *knew* or *should have known* ("actual" versus "constructive" knowledge) about a worker being harassed, retaliated against, or the like, you have an affirmative obligation to intercede. The icon of the monkey covering its eyes, ears, and mouth—that is, not wanting to know what was going on around it—won't hold up in court and will do little to sustain positive employee relations at work. In court, your organization is treated as a corporate citizen, and questions will be raised as to whether that "citizen" acted responsibly and appropriately by interceding on behalf of its most vulnerable and disadvantaged members.

Further, supervisors, managers, and officers of a company are required to affirmatively disclose any and all complaints regarding potential harassment, discrimination, retaliation, or workplace violence without exception—even if the complaining employee asks that no investigation be conducted. Managers cannot and should never promise confidentiality in matters relating to discrimination, harassment, or potential violence in the workplace—period. So, if someone asks you to "talk off the record," respond this way:

I'm not sure I can do that: it depends on the issue. If what you're about to tell me has to do with discrimination, harassment, retaliation, the possibility of violence in the workplace, or if it has to do with a potential conflict of interest with the company as a whole, I'll have to escalate and disclose that. I can't keep that confidential. That being said, I can tell you that we'll make reasonable efforts to keep the matter confidential and on a strict need-to-know basis. Still, depending on the nature of the complaint, I may have a legal and ethical duty to bring the matter to HR, compliance, or our in-house counsel. I also want to remind you that our company maintains a strict antiretaliation policy that protects employees who lodge complaints made in good faith. With all that being said, can we sit and talk?

In short, this is a "melting ice cube syndrome," and you don't have the discretion to keep secrets or maintain confidences once someone places you on notice that they feel harassed: the quicker you address, escalate, and resolve the issue, the better. Equally, watch out for land mines when someone from outside your group who reports to someone else complains about their supervisor. No matter how much you want to help, you'll be setting yourself and the organization up for failure if the issue surrounds harassment, retaliation, discrimination, or similar allegations. In such cases, convince the individual to speak with her supervisor, offer to accompany her to do so, or escalate the matter to HR yourself. Whatever you opt to do, keeping the matter confidential is *not* one of your options in such circumstances!

Next, understand the broader, loosely defined definitions that employees may throw your way when bringing up complaints. Many times, they're not quite aware of what these terms actually mean in the legal sense, but they drop them like bombs hoping to intimidate management by threatening a lawsuit. Following are some short definitions of the terms that drive much employment litigation and that you should understand at a high level:

Discrimination: Employment discrimination is a form of discrimination based on an employee's actual or perceived "membership" in a protected classification, including, for example, race, sex, sexual orientation, religion, national origin, physical or mental disability, or age. Many states have their own discrimination protection laws and categories that typically exceed those identified under federal law. A "disparate treatment" claim arises when employees or applicants allege that they were treated differently in terms and conditions of employment based on protected characteristics or any other factors that are not legitimate business reasons.

Harassment: Harassment is a subset of employment discrimination and generally is defined as subjecting an employee to unfavorable working conditions because of the employee's actual or perceived membership in a protected classification, without business justification. Workplace harassment complaints are divided into two areas:

- ■ **"Hostile Work Environment" Claims:** A form of harassment that may be severe or pervasive or that otherwise negatively impacts the conditions of the employee/victim's work environment. Hostile work environment claims make up approximately 90–95 percent of all harassment issues that make their way into the litigation arena. The harassment must be unwanted (that is, offensive to the recipient and to a reasonable person in the employee's situation). A hostile work environment can be sexual but can also be based on race, sex, religion, national origin, color, disability, sexual orientation, age, and other protected categories.
- ■ **"Quid Pro Quo" Claims:** A Latin term meaning "this for that," quid pro quo harassment typically only makes up less than 10 percent of harassment claims and is often depicted by the "casting couch" scenario: for the starlet to get the part in

the movie, she must sleep with the casting director. Quid pro quo harassment is a form of harassment in which a supervisor, or someone who has authority over the employee, conditions the terms of employment upon sexual behavior (for example, dating and physical sex) and in which a tangible job detriment (such as, poor performance review, demotion, or termination) occurs when the employee refuses to cooperate.

Retaliation: Retaliation may occur when an employee's terms and conditions of employment are negatively affected because he or she complained about someone within the company, refused to go along with conduct that the employee deemed to be unethical or a violation of the law, or served as a witness against the company regarding claims of discrimination, harassment, or other violations of law or public policy.

Discrimination, harassment, and retaliation are very alive and well in corporate America. Whether you're a passive investigator in a claim by the nature of your leadership role within your company or you're "on the sharp end of the investigation spear" because the claims are being levied against you personally, simply remember this: follow the lead investigator's instructions as closely as possible. That lead investigator may be your human resources representative, employee or labor relations director, or an outside consultant or attorney. Whatever the case, such claims have the potential to garner significant liability against the company and could result in a corporate leader's "summary discharge"—meaning an immediate termination without prior steps of progressive discipline or corrective action.

Let's look at an unfortunate but all-too-common example, which will serve as a cautionary tale and show how summary discharges often result in cases of supervisors dating subordinates without disclosing the relationship to management.

An administrative assistant reports to human resources unannounced one day and states that she can no longer take it. She's been sleeping with her boss, the VP of operations, for nine months, and she knows it was wrong because he's married. But she felt compelled to do so for fear of retaliation if she didn't submit to his advances. The HR person takes the claimant's story and makes detailed notes by listening openly to the administrative assistant's claims. HR then wisely sends her home on an investigatory leave with pay so that HR can notify the appropriate parties (for example, higher levels of HR, in-house legal, and the VP of operations' immediate supervisor, the chief operations officer) and prepare to launch an impartial investigation without her present on company premises.

Once HR has escalated this claim to the appropriate parties and developed an investigational game plan and strategy, HR and the COO call in the VP of operations to explain the nature of the allegation and learn his side of the story. Lo and behold, he readily admits to having a nine-month-long affair with his assistant but claims that it was purely consensual. "We both fell in love with each other, my marriage is on the rocks, and I don't know why she's coming forward to disclose this to you because it's a private matter just between the two of us" goes the typical executive response.

With this he said/she said scenario in place and the female subordinate likely reaching out to an attorney to claim quid pro quo harassment, the company swiftly decides to terminate the VP of operations. First, the investigation isn't able to prove much beyond her stating that she felt compelled to engage in sex for fear of retaliation and his stating that their affair was consensual. Second, under most organizations' codes of conduct or employee handbooks, the supervisor is the primary party responsible for disclosing a romantic relationship with a subordinate. Failure to do so typically warrants "summary dismissal" in cases like these because of the tremendous liability that such nondisclosures entail (as this case study proves). Third, the organization must immediately protect itself from further legal liability by showing that it acted as a responsible corporate citizen in terminating the supervisor as soon as it learned of the problem so as to mitigate the damage. And fourth, the organization must uphold the integrity of its mission statement by providing a safe and healthy workplace for its workers at all times.

As a result, the VP of operations is fired pretty much on the spot, and the company is now on the hook for the administrative assistant's potential claims of harassment under the legal concept of "strict liability." Strict liability posits that a company may be automatically ("strictly") liable for the acts of its managers in cases of harassment simply by the nature of the role and responsibilities they hold as leaders and regardless of their intentions or any negligence or fault on their part.

It even gets worse for that VP of operations: if the executive attended harassment training, code of conduct training, and signed off on the employee handbook that likely addressed discrimination, harassment, and the obligation to disclose personal, romantic relationships that develop with subordinates, those all serve as proof that the company acted responsibly and demonstrated that the executive unilaterally acted "outside the course and scope of his employment."

As such, the company can then look to shift liability toward the defendant (the former VP of operations) and away from the company, thereby mitigating the company's legal exposure. Unfortunately, that means that the former VP of operations could be sued personally for such "managerial bad acts." In many states, individual managers can be sued for up to $50,000 of their own money for such transgressions; in other states like California, however, there is no monetary cap. Yikes!

It's important that you, as an organizational leader, understand the role of training, your organization's code of conduct (in terms of disclosing romantic relationships that develop with subordinates), and your company's probable course of action should you ever fail to disclose such a romantic relationship. Simply know that an accusation of "consensual" versus "forced" sexual relations can very easily be made by a subordinate against a supervisor, and it works all ways: female versus male, male versus female, male versus male, and female versus female. This "cautionary tale" is all too real for executives who risk such behaviors. Simply put, they don't pay you enough to risk your personal savings and your financial security for such indiscretions!

ETHICAL LEADERSHIP AND SUSTAINING A MORAL WORKPLACE

A NEW WAY FORWARD

21

LESSONS FROM THE HR TRENCHES AND WISDOM FOR THE AGES

E very book has its vantage point. Writers engage a particular subject by their own sets of experiences and the results they derived from them. After spending the better part of three decades in the HR trenches, I've written this book from the vantage point of senior HR leadership. And while that may sound insightful and fascinating on the one hand, it also can become wearying watching well-intentioned managers stepping on land mines left and right. HR, when done right, demonstrates and models effective leadership, superior communication, and well-executed teamwork. Moreover, it's looked to as the department that fosters healthy morale, ethics, and professional development. Many would argue that HR, more so than any other department, reflects the organization's heart and soul.

Most HR executives and practitioners wish they could just get out there in front of the parade and steer people away from the cliff and away from the peril and drama that comes with supervising workers on a daily basis. So many of the silly errors that HR witnesses are avoidable, especially the ones that create a legal record that get both the company and individual manager in trouble.

Hence the purpose of this book: to assist frontline leaders in strengthening their communication skills, awareness, and general approach to managing successfully. Following are a few key strategies and tips that will arguably help you avoid the plaintiff's lawyer's snare and, more importantly, become and remain a standout leader whom people will rally behind.

IT'S OKAY TO TAKE THINGS "OUTSIDE THE FAMILY"

Too many managers don't want to take their department's problems "outside the family" and share their concerns with HR (or some other neutral function within the company). Instead, they hog all the problems to themselves and sometimes go as far as threatening team members that if they go to HR to file a complaint, they'll be fired. There's probably no greater leadership shortcoming. Creating a public record that you'll retaliate against anyone who lodges a good faith complaint with the company's ombudsman could very well land an executive leader or frontline supervisor on the sharp end of the investigation spear. Outright termination or at least a final written warning could be warranted, even for a first offense.

After all, when you've got a computer problem on your hands, there's absolutely no shame in picking up the phone to call the help desk. Ah, but if you have a people problem, calling HR is risky, isn't it? First, they may make matters worse by launching some big investigation. Or it could ruin your reputation if it gets around that you can't handle the people problems on your team, right? In fact, that's why you're in management—to resolve problems and ensure that your team is productive.

Nonsense! When you've got a people problem, get that hot potato off your lap! If you're fortunate enough to have an HR department, remember that that's what they're there for. *Run, don't walk,* to HR when you've got a performance problem on your hands, and share that priority with the department that's there to help you. (If your organization does not have an HR department, escalate matters to your supervisor.) HR has likely seen this all before, and making HR a partner on the front end gives you an ally and objective resource to help you navigate the rapids of what might come your way. It also makes the best record should something proceed to litigation at some point.

Likewise, HR can help you avoid some of the rookie mistakes made by managers who may not realize that they're being set up for a preemptive strike or some other type of trap that's laid before them. Don't take on the world alone—it's too burdensome and hazardous a route. And don't forget that the cards are somewhat stacked against you, the big, bad employer (at least in the eyes of a jury of the worker's peers, who generally relate much more to a poor, terminated employee than to a member of management). In fact, many workers are even being coached by plaintiffs' lawyers while they're still employed and working for you. So, give yourself every advantage by partnering with the team that's designed to help you lead more effectively and avoid land mines that may otherwise explode underneath you.

DON'T ASSUME YOU HAVE TO BE FEARED TO LEAD EFFECTIVELY

Female leaders often fall prey to the common thinking that you have to be mean, tough, fierce, or otherwise feared to compete in a man's world. So do newly minted supervisors. Ditto for lots of male leaders, for that matter. Their reasoning? If people don't fear you to some degree, you won't be respected or otherwise effective in your role. They'll take advantage of you every step of the way if you're too nice. Again, nonsense! Some of the most effective leaders in corporate America at all levels are beloved and adored. They're seen as nurturers, good listeners, and empathetic and selfless human beings. The secret to their success doesn't lie in their ability to instill fear in others—it lies in their ability to make others better human beings. And people feel that sense of specialness when dealing with leaders like these. They sense their genuineness, their true love of people and their work, and their willingness to help others better themselves.

Jim Collins, in his bestselling book *Good to Great,* referred to these individuals as "Level 5 Leaders"—those who combine humility with great determination to become enduring influences on people's lives.

Maya Angelou, the renowned American poet, famously stated: "I've learned that people will forget what you said, people will forget what you did, but people will never forget how you made them feel."

It's by no means that these angels that enter our lives from time to time have to be an anomaly. The purpose of this book is to inspire you to become that very kind of leader yourself—someone who engages and motivates others to become the best they can be, someone whose leadership style and genuineness penetrates people's hearts as well as their minds. It's by no means impossible to live this type of leadership life. In fact, it's all around you. The question you have to ask yourself is, who are you in light of this concept called *selfless leadership,* and who do you choose to be? Like everything else in life, you're the first domino. You can make the change to becoming an inspirational leader by simply changing your fundamental thought about being so.

For those who doubt this approach because it sounds too good to be true or too Pollyanna-ish, simply think about the worst consequences that can come of this leadership style: people won't respect you and will constantly take advantage of you. Okay, to a degree, that may be true—at least initially. But selfless leaders put others' needs ahead of their own and expect others to respond in kind. And the beauty of human nature is that people typically do. They'll sense your authenticity and selflessness and put your needs (and the company's needs) ahead of their own. And they won't do it out of some form of fear or compliance—they'll do it simply because they want to. They'll sense that you treat them with respect, hold them accountable like adults, and teach them so they can grow and develop in their own careers. And in feeling good about themselves because of your enlightened leadership style, they'll give discretionary effort more than they otherwise would out of loyalty and pride. Greatness can be found at the margin of output in the form of additional energy, effort, and goodwill. That may sound like a small thing when you're looking at one worker, but think about the difference it could make when a department or an entire company is coming from that orientation!

What about the occasional staffer who tries to take advantage of your good nature? It may go on for a little while, but before too long, peer influence will typically fix the problem as peers "realign" that coworker's errant approach to your leadership style. "Hey, knock it off. Paul deserves better than that, and he'd never treat you or any of us that way. I see what you're doing and don't like it. So does everyone else, including Paul. This isn't going to work for you if you keep it up." And the beauty of this healthy and "self-repairing" ecosystem is that you'll have created an environment where even the problem children straighten themselves out because you'll have lifted up those around them. This isn't la-la land by any means. It's very real and practical, and it's working for thousands of leaders out there just like you. Our goal, then, is simply to turn the light on so that this type of selfless leadership is no longer rare or an exception. To compete effectively in corporate America in the twenty-first century, companies and their leaders will have to make the employment experience more personal and intimate. It's simply the next step in our nation's commercial development and workplace history, and it's a long-awaited and practical change that will help ethical organizations compete by retaining the best and brightest talent.

22

DIVERSITY, EQUITY, AND INCLUSION
A MISSION-CRITICAL BUSINESS IMPERATIVE

Diversity, equity, and inclusion (DEI) are such critical parts of any organization's business strategy. McKinsey and other consulting firms, as well as myriad business schools, have confirmed that organizations with diverse boards, leadership teams, and workforces continue to outperform companies with more homogeneous employee and board constituents. DEI covers such a broad swath of business areas, so let's look at some of the ways of expanding your program to recruit, retain, develop, and promote individuals of all kinds. After all, even without all the proof from management consultants and research universities, it's simply good sense to ensure your employee and board populations reflect the demographic characteristics of your consumers, customers, and clients.

Using the strategy behind Atul Gawande's bestselling and highly lauded book *The Checklist Manifesto,* we can cover the broadest swath of topic areas using a template that captures the breadth and depth of such a critical initiative. We know that some of the world's most critical interactions succeed with the help of a simple checklist methodology. Airlines require that pilots employ checklists before every flight. Surgeons often scan checklists before initiating certain complicated procedures. Leading executive coaches like Marshall Goldsmith in his Stakeholder Centered Executive Coaching program recommend checklists before each client engagement and use them themselves to ensure they're on point and covering all their bases. So, whether you're analyzing employee demographics, recruitment statistics, retention and promotion records, or marketing and customer data, a checklist may make sense in terms of initiating and strengthening your organization's DEI programs and initiatives as well.

A STARTING POINT

This is not meant to assume that something as important as DEI can be limited to a checklist by any means. For purposes of this book, however, the checklist template helps demonstrate the broad breadth and reach of DEI so that readers can appreciate its vast applications. Understanding the diversity of the local (or extended) community you serve—where your consumers, customers, and clients reside, and their demographic makeup—is a great place to begin. For example, if your business is located in the San Fernando Valley outside Los Angeles, your local demographic makeup might look like this: 42 percent Hispanic, 41 percent White, 12 percent Asian, and 5 percent Black. Why is that important? Because you want to understand the makeup of the community you serve and have a measuring rod against which to base your employee demographic analysis. Obtaining this information is fairly easy with a simple Google search or with the help of the local chamber of commerce or economic development corporation.

Of course, DEI extends far beyond race and gender to include, among other things, age, disability, sexual orientation, veteran status, and more. That being said, establishing a baseline of the community you serve and where your establishment is located is a great place to start. Internal diversity metrics will then help you gain a snapshot of your own company's demographics. Finally, understanding how to attract more diverse talent pools makes for a simple baseline against which you can measure progress toward your organization's diversity, equity, and inclusion efforts. Again, this is only meant to be a launching point, as DEI is far more complex and intricate than a simple checklist template might otherwise indicate. But if you're looking to truly delve into this critical study and analysis, benchmarking local and company demographics is an excellent place to start.

THE TEMPLATE

A checklist that measures human capital isn't intended to be static. It's intended to change, adapt, and evolve as new insights become available and warrant further exploration. But keeping it simple initially makes the most sense, while allowing the checklist to expand on its own as new data creates additional opportunities.

DIVERSITY, EQUITY, AND INCLUSION (DEI) CHECKLIST TEMPLATE	
Local Worker and Extended Customer Demographics	Research statistics regarding your local workplace community and, more importantly, the customers and consumers you serve. Start with ethnicity, age, gender, gender orientation/LGTBQIA+*, veteran, and disability statistics, if available.
Company Workforce Statistics	Analyze your current workforce demography by location, including ethnicity, age, gender, gender orientation, veteran, disability status, and other critical factors.
Company Diversity Metrics	Review the following metrics for the particular aspects of diversity orientation that you're focusing on (for example, age, gender, ethnicity): (1) retention rate; (2) internal job fill ratio; (3) promotion rate; (4) turnover percentage, including involuntary versus voluntary turnover.
Employee Life Cycle Analysis and Talent Diversity	Measure each of the following key gateways and paths closely to determine where diversity tends to "fall off": (1) applicant sourcing, (2) interview screening, (3) hiring, (4) retention, (5) internal mobility, and (6) succession planning. Look for trends and patterns in roadblock areas and build your recruitment and retention programs as well as your exit interviews purposely around those challenges.

Recruitment Advertising Outreach Sources	Expand your typical Indeed.com and LinkedIn sourcing methods to include DiversityJobs.com, LatinoJobs.org, OverFiftyJobs.com, DisabilityJobs.net, AsianHires.com, NativeJobs.org, LGBTjobsite.com, VeteranJobs.net, BlackCareers.org, and WeHireWomen.com. Niche sites won't produce the volume of big job boards, but the quality of candidates should justify the cost of the ads.
Talent Intelligence (AI-Driven) Platforms	Talent intelligence (artificial intelligence–driven) platforms are becoming commercially available to identify internal talent and align succession planning and high potential development. AI can search for adjacent skills and focus on the potential of each individual applicant or employee. AI can mask individuals' identities and reduce unconscious bias. AI analytics can point to underrepresented groups that drop off within the hiring cycle or the internal promotion process. AI can "learn" diversity metrics to better achieve diversity goals, so long as they're updated, monitored, and adjusted regularly.

*The LGBTQ+ acronym is formed based on the following terms: lesbian, gay, bisexual, transgender, and queer. It's also common to see the acronym LGBTQQIA+ used nowadays, expanded for a clearer representation of lesbian, gay, bisexual, transgender, queer, questioning, intersex, and asexual people. The addition of the "+" symbol indicates its expansive meaning and stands for love, acceptance, and the embracing of all.

THE "QUALITY FOUR"

Of course, no template is broad enough to cover the essence and quality of your organization's hiring, retention, and promotion programs. Checklists, however, can certainly help on the quantitative side to ensure that you're touching all the bases and the key elements of a successful program. On the qualitative side, look to the following four broad categories as a good place to start:

- **Workforce DEI**. Hiring, retaining, developing, and promoting a diversity of employees
- **Workplace DEI**: Creating a company culture rooted in acceptance and belonging
- **Marketplace DEI**: Attracting and delighting a diversity of customers and suppliers
- **Community DEI**: Contributing to all parts of the community a company serves

Only a broad and holistic approach that incorporates all four stakeholders above will make for a true DEI program worthy of your organization and your employees. Make no mistake, however: diversity, equity, and inclusion are not options; they are business imperatives. DEI is essential for successful business organizations to drive innovation, achieve business results, and realize sustainable growth. Developing a DEI policy and corresponding company initiatives that help achieve a truly diverse, equitable, and inclusive organization is an ethical yet practical endeavor. It's proven to be a critical "must have" for attracting and retaining Millennial and Gen-Z workers, along with environmentalism and giving back to the community by fulfilling a corporation's social responsibility. You don't need to have a perfect start—you just need to start. See if a simple checklist template approach helps you build and develop your program over time to capture broader and more nuanced aspects of your organization's commitment to this critical business and ethical imperative.

Special Note: Employee Resource Groups, or ERGs, are voluntary, employee-led groups that typically share a common characteristic (like gender, ethnicity, religious affiliation, lifestyle, or personal interests) and form to foster a more diverse and inclusive workplace aligned with their values. There is often no better way to lobby for your interests—whether they be corporate social responsibility, environmental sustainability, military-to-veteran transition, or a diverse workforce—than in partnership with friends and peers. All it takes is some dedication and time on your part to form and lead such a group. The results can be amazing and exceptionally self-fulfilling.

23

EDUCATING ENTRY-LEVEL AND NONEXEMPT WORKERS ON ETHICAL ISSUES THEY MAY OTHERWISE MISS

As with all things having to do with successful leadership, communication, and teambuilding, it's the little things you do that count. Whether you're hiring recent high school or college graduates, take the time to teach them what they don't learn in school: the ethical rules of the road. Far too many young adults have entered the workforce without the proper introduction and education, only to find themselves on the sharp end of the investigation spear and terminated for cause—without realizing why until it was too late. Raise expectations by heightening awareness early on and engaging your earlier career workers in all matters relating to career growth and development. Teach them life lessons when they join your organization—arguably their first encounter with a full-time job and the sometimes-harsh realities of the workplace. More importantly, steer them clear of mistaken assumptions that may have landed their predecessors in hot water for failing to understand that school and workplace realities can differ significantly.

MISTAKEN ASSUMPTION #1:
"If I mess up, the company has to give me written notice before they can fire me, right?"

Wrong! In all states except Montana, new hires are technically hired "at will," meaning that a company can terminate them with or without cause or notice. (Montana is the only state that requires just cause to terminate an employee outside of the probationary period.) Further, most organizations have "introductory" periods, otherwise known as "probationary" periods, which allow them to terminate a new hire at whim if that person isn't meeting performance or conduct standards. In fact, even if you're hired into a union job, most collective bargaining agreements give employers full latitude to terminate at whim within the probationary period (typically sixty to ninety days). So it's definitely not the case that you're entitled to some form of documented corrective action before a company will feel comfortable pulling the plug on your employment.

MISTAKEN ASSUMPTION #2:
Companies treat performance problems the same way they treat conduct problems.

Wrong again! Performance and conduct challenges are typically handled in a totally different manner in most organizations. When you think of "progressive discipline" (aka "corrective action") in the form of a verbal, written, and ultimately final written warning, you're usually referring to performance or attendance problems. But conduct or behavior-based infractions often warrant what's known as "summary dismissal" (that is, immediate termination)— even for a first offense.

It's easy enough to understand why a company would terminate someone outright for theft, embezzlement, fraud, and the like, but employees don't realize that there are other types of infractions that typically result in immediate dismissal as well. Here are just a few:

Timecard Fraud

In the workplace, time is a proxy for money. If you steal time, it's the same as stealing money, because the end result is the same: the company is out the money that you took illegally. For example, if you put in for overtime that you didn't work, that's considered "timecard fraud." You may not have stolen $10 from the cash register, but the ultimate effect is the same: you're $10 richer at the company's expense. Likewise, if you arrive at work two hours late but falsify your timecard to show that you arrived on time, you'll be awarding yourself two hours of additional straight time pay. Again, companies will likely view this as theft, plain and simple.

Further, employers don't have much wiggle room *not* to terminate in cases like these. After all, the new hire will have left them little choice: not terminating after an egregious act like theft (or timecard fraud, in this case) could create an unwanted precedent. And it would be difficult for a company not to terminate Employee A but then later argue they are going to terminate Employee B for the same offense. In short, when it comes to conduct infractions, the issue drives the outcome: no matter how much they like you, love you, or adore you, if you engage in egregious misconduct, the company will have no option but to terminate you for cause—even for a first occurrence. Think of it as a "third rail" metaphor: no matter how long someone has been with a company or how stellar the individual's record, if they step on the third rail of a train track, they'll be reduced to a piece of bacon. No forgiveness and no exceptions.

Casual Drug Use

What workers do in their private time is generally up to them, but personal activities can sometimes unwittingly bleed into the workplace. For example, many companies have a "for cause" drug-testing standard that requires anyone involved in a slip-and-fall incident or auto accident to be tested for cause. Here's how it works. Say your general duties include driving a company vehicle and you're rear-ended at a stop sign across the street from the office. While it certainly wasn't your fault that someone rear-ended your company car while you were at a full stop, the fact that you were officially involved in an auto accident may require that you be tested for drug usage. (Many companies' policies don't distinguish fault in situations like these—an employee's involvement is enough to trigger the drug test.)

As it turns out, about two weeks ago at your twenty-second birthday party, you smoked marijuana with your friends. Unfortunately, you didn't realize that pot stays in your bloodstream for about thirty days, and low and behold, you test positive for drugs. The end result? You're terminated for failing to abide by your company's drug and alcohol abuse policy, even though the effects of the pot have long since disappeared. No, life isn't always fair, but you're a working adult now, and you have to understand and be held accountable for the ramifications of your decisions and actions.

Employment Application Falsification

If you're four units short of your bachelor's but show on your resume and employment application that you already have a degree, you'll find yourself back in the unemployment line before you know it. Why? Because you falsified your preemployment record to give yourself an unfair advantage that helped you land the job . . . even though it was based on false pretenses. The alternative:

create the proper record on your resume and employment application showing that you're four units short of your bachelor's degree. Any falsification of your employment credentials may get you terminated weeks or months after you began in your new role once the company finds out. Again, it's nothing personal: they simply can't risk creating an unwanted precedent by not terminating you for material falsification of your employment application.

The lesson: companies terminate swiftly and consistently when it comes to ethics breaches and dishonesty. Put another way, conduct- and behavior-related infractions provide companies the discretion to skip any steps of written, corrective action and escalate immediately and directly to the termination stage. And the downside for you, of course, is twofold: First, you'll have lost your current job. Second, you'll have a much more difficult time during an interview with a prospective employer when you're asked why you left your previous company. (Hint: "I was terminated for cause due to an ethical breach and violation of the company's code of conduct" isn't a great lead-in when you're in job search mode.)

It's simple but still as true as ever: always tell the truth. Don't take shortcuts, especially when it comes to electronic records that can be easily traced in an audit (which companies do all the time). Be cautious of casual drug use. And, most important, create a reputation for yourself early in your career as an ethical worker who demonstrates the highest level of integrity. It will help you avoid common pitfalls like the ones above and sleep better at night as you build your career and grow and develop in your role.

MISTAKEN ASSUMPTION #3:
No One's Watching

As with most things in life, people watch you more than you know. That means you have a greater influence on others than you could ever dream of. How do you know that's so? When people come up to you years later and thank you for some small nicety that you did for them that you can't even remember, you begin to realize just how much you touch others' lives. That's just how the universe is designed, and that's always where your greatest opportunities lie.

Everyone's always watching you. That's not some Orwellian concept to make you nervous or paranoid. It's a grand insight and understanding about how important you are to everyone around you, both in the workplace and in your life overall. Do you really want to get ahead in your career as you launch into the workplace? Simply follow these three simple rules:

1. Smile. Create a welcoming environment so that others feel comfortable approaching you and feel drawn to you.

2. Go out of your way to provide outstanding customer service to everyone you come in contact with. Show that you care in everything you do. People respect competence, but they love even more dealing with someone who's passionate and excited about their work.

3. Look for opportunities to assume greater responsibilities. Everyone needs an additional set of hands and extra help from time to time—everyone. Be there for them. Develop a reputation for ethics and integrity. Take on more, assist wherever and whenever you can, and become the "go-to" person for anyone needing additional support. All you have to do is ask.

These three simple rules will catapult your career to new heights. You'll make new friends and strong networking contacts. You'll gain exposure to opportunities you won't otherwise have known about. And you'll have fun doing it. Be the role model for others to follow. Set the bar for others when it comes to ethics and trust. Go that extra mile to help. Then let your strategy pay off in spades as good things come your way for all the positive energy you place into the universe. Always remember how special you are and what a gift your work offers you to define and rebrand yourself and give back to others.

24

ETHICS IS PERSONAL

A SAMPLE HOLLYWOOD SCRIPT TO LIVE BY

Besides being an author, I'm a human resources executive. I've spent a good part of my career close to television production, both at Paramount Pictures and Nickelodeon. People often ask me what it's like working in "TV land," and I always say how much I've enjoyed it. But people are people—plain and simple. In fact, few know this, but at the beginning of every new production season, the casts and crews of all your favorite TV productions have to undergo "respect in the workplace" training (that is, antidiscrimination and antiharassment overviews). Everyone in the industry knows that working on a "toxic set" can be a miserable way to make a living and even lead to high-profile publicity and lawsuits. Studios have figured out that placing antiharassment training at the beginning of each new production season is smart business because it sets the guidelines clearly and simply from day one—getting everyone on the same page right from the start in terms of behavioral expectations and land mines that should be avoided at all costs.

Usually an attorney leads the training (it's California, after all!), with production leadership sitting right in the front row to chime in when necessary. Some attorneys and production heads do this type of presentation better than others, but here's one that I heard that always left an impression on me. It was from my days on the Paramount lot, and while this isn't a word-for-word translation, it's from the notes I took listening to a production head who was clearly an outstanding leader. Listen in and see if you can adopt a similar tale to share with your teams that they can relate to and make their own.

Everyone, I want to chime in here as the executive producer. The broader question that I want to tag on our attorney's wisdom and guidance is what can be done about a toxic work environment? Seriously. Not just the proverbial "memo from the front office" telling us how we should get along and accept one another's differences, opinions, and "worldviews." Not just the in-house or visiting employment attorneys who lead the preproduction antidiscrimination/sexual harassment training on the production sets at the start of every new TV season. They present facts. This needs to be about spirit. This needs to register on an emotional level to make a true difference. Addressing it proactively can make a real and lasting impact. If we're going to do this right, it has got to become personal. It needs to emanate from your very being as a leader and role model, which each person in this room is. It's got to be addressed verbally today but written in stone in your heart. And it's got to remain a check-in topic from time to time, not just something we address annually or at the start of a new production season.

First, a quick tale. Many of you may remember the TV shows from the '70s *Happy Days* and *Laverne and Shirley*. (Those of you too young to remember can watch them in syndication.) Both were produced by legendary TV guru Garry Marshall. They were shot right next door to one another on Stages 19 and 20, respectively, here on the Paramount lot. Laverne, Penny Marshall, was actually

Garry Marshall's sister in real life. So you'd think he'd have a pref-
erence for *Laverne and Shirley* over *Happy Days*. It turns out that
wasn't the case at all. In his book, *My Happy Days in Hollywood,*
Garry describes how well everyone got along on the set of *Happy
Days*. Ron Howard was like a son to him, the younger actors respected the older ones like parents, and everyone had one another's
backs. Set visits were encouraged for publicity reasons, and the cast
got along about as well as any team in Hollywood TV history.

Not so with *Laverne and Shirley*. The two leads were self-
described prima donnas; they cursed like sailors, they fired the
writing team, only to hire and fire another, until it got to the point
where no one wanted to be associated with that show or its cast for
fear it could damage them professionally. Set visits were avoided
because the next blowup was always right around the corner, and
the drama never ended. Suffice it to say they were successful despite
the toxic environment that everyone had to endure. I want our production to mirror *Happy Days*, not *Laverne and Shirley*.

I want us to enjoy coming to work. I want us to create memories
for ourselves and for one another that we'll be celebrating twenty
and thirty years from now. I want you to be able to live and experience Andy Bernard's greatest quote from the last episode of *The
Office*: "I wish there was a way to know you're in the good old days
before you've actually left them." It all starts with you and the expectations you should have for yourself and for everyone else on
our team.

It's that simple. I can't mandate happiness and that people like
one another, but I can set a very high bar in terms of the ethical
behaviors and conduct that I expect from everyone on this crew in
terms of how you treat one another. You're all exceptionally tal-
ented to make the cut and be part of this team, but talent and hard
work alone are only half of what you'll need to be successful and

remain here. You're equally responsible for ensuring that the entire team enjoys working with you and seeks out your guidance when they have questions or need help. That's the standard I'm looking for. No other behavioral traits are necessary or needed from this point forward as part of this team. Simply throw any misconceptions out of your head, remove them from your toolbox, and determine how you can be part of the solution in terms of creating a friendly, inclusive, and fun work environment.

While I appreciate the formal legal training and the memo regarding policy acknowledgment that you all have to sign, I want you all to hear directly from me on this first day of production that nothing less than professionalism, respect, and selfless leadership is what I expect to see each day without exception. Seeing how well it works, seeing how much productivity and creativity springs from a healthy work environment where you can do your best work every day, will help us stand out now and help you all flourish in your future.

Let's have fun. Let's keep it light. Let's not fall into the trap of taking ourselves too seriously. But most important, let's make sure that everyone feels like they've got a seat at the table—no matter what their role. We're all one team. One production. One class that's wise enough to follow the professor's lead when it comes to something as important as our behavior, conduct, and attitude. Now you've heard what I expect of you. Now you know. Does anyone have any questions or suggestions at this point? [*No.*] Great.

Then combined with the antidiscrimination training that we've all received and that memo from the front office in which you have to acknowledge that you're required to follow specific policies, know that our verbal agreement right now sets the tone for the whole season, lifts us up to do our best work and bring our best game to this set every day, and helps us create our own happy days that we'll be able to celebrate for the rest of our lives.

Simply stated. Simply put. An ethical commitment like this from any leader in any environment will go a long way in creating and sustaining a healthy culture and work environment that everyone can be proud of. There is no need to make this any harder or more complicated than by simply voicing your commitment and making it a basic part of your team's belief system. Respect begets accountability. Accountability feeds commitment. Commitment drives results. And you can have fun along the way.

THERE'S SO MUCH MORE TO ETHICS

YOU WON'T WANT TO MISS THIS!

Workplace ethics focuses on the conduct and moral challenges you'll likely face in the workplace as a leader, manager, or executive. But corporate ethics is a much broader area than what you'll typically find in the office or on the shop floor at any given time. Therefore, this will serve as a quick overview of some of the broader aspects that will likewise inform you about the critical nature of ethics in a larger business context.

INSIDER INFORMATION AND CONFIDENTIALITY

There are several critical rules of the road regarding "insider trading" and corporate confidentiality that are important to share, as federal securities laws are complex, and violators face criminal penalties:

1. Information learned at work stays at work.
2. Share information that you learn at work only on a need-to-know basis.
3. Prevent inadvertent disclosure of confidential information that might otherwise mistakenly be shared via email, texting, or in an elevator.

4. You may not trade securities (typically stocks and bonds or other financial instruments) based on "material" information not available to the public (that is, insider trading).

5. When in doubt, check with your supervisor, a company attorney, or your internal corporate compliance officer.

COMMUNICATION WITH THE NEWS MEDIA

Rule: only official spokespersons may speak to the press about your company.

1. Corporate relations, public relations, corporate communications, or another designated internal department is the only group that may speak with the media, other than the CEO or another designated member of senior management.

2. If you don't know who that person is, it isn't you.

3. Refer all requests to corporate relations or to your company attorney.

4. Be careful about speaking in public about company business, whether on the record or off.

5. Be cautious of casual conversations at social gatherings.

6. Clear any speeches or presentations made outside the company.

7. State that your views are not those of your company.

8. When in doubt, call your supervisor, corporate/public relations department, or company attorney even for discussions of noncompany business.

ANTITRUST AND COMPETITION

Antitrust and trade practice laws are designed to preserve a competitive economy in which free enterprise can flourish. Such laws protect competition, protect consumers, and foster and reward innovation. Antitrust laws are complex, and penalties are severe, so always consult with legal when questions arise.

Along these lines, remain cognizant of relations with competitors. For example, price fixing is prohibited. That means that you may never exchange sales lists or attempt to set market prices with competitors. Only your company alone determines prices in light of costs, market conditions, and other factors. Along these same lines, there can be no allocation of markets for customers, territories, or lines of product. Any such agreement would be, per se, unlawful. If you're in a meeting with peers and these types of conversations come up, walk out and call your company's lawyer to explain the conflict.

COMPENSATION AND THE "PRICE OF LABOR"

Special Note: "Compensation" is considered the "price of labor." Therefore, it is impermissible to reach out to competitor organizations to conduct your own salary survey. Surveys may be published from third-party resources. Or consultants may be hired to conduct confidential surveys, the results of which are shared blindly with participating companies. But you never want to send an email to contacts at competitor organizations asking, "Can anyone tell me how much you're paying salary range–wise for a director of human resources with three direct reports?" or anything similar. That kind of email can get you in trouble for literally costing the price of labor with competitors, potentially violating federal price fixing laws.

When it comes to customers and suppliers, your company may do business with, or refuse to do business with, anyone it chooses. However, companies cannot refuse to do business with certain groups for discriminatory reasons. Decisions must be made by your organization independently for legitimate business reasons. Here's what's important: no refusal to do business can be made in concert with a third party (for example, a competitor) to squeeze a third-party organization, such as a vendor or supplier, out of business.

Further, antitrust laws may prohibit certain kinds of long-term or exclusive deals. For example, agreements to purchase all supplies from one particular dealer, agreements to buy the entire output of one company, certain reciprocal dealing agreements, or conditioning the sale of one product on the purchase of another (a concept known as "tying") may be deemed unlawful. In other words, you can't cooperate with your competition to disadvantage third parties or promise "you-wash-my-back-and-I'll-wash-yours" types of sales arrangements with competitors.

Finally, seek the guidance of your company lawyer when engaging in any sales activities that could appear to violate antitrust laws. For example, you may not dictate resale prices, impose territorial restrictions, or tie the sale of one of your company's products to the purchase of another one of your products. In short, you cannot discriminate in the pricing of goods or services between two or more competing customers so as to reduce competition.

POLITICAL CONTRIBUTIONS

Rule: company assets may not be used improperly to influence government officials.

While you're welcome to make personal contributions or engage in political activity for personal reasons, understand that your company will not reimburse you for individual contributions.

Companies will typically not make federal political contributions except through their own political action committee, or PAC.

Typically, a company's office of government affairs, or OGA, must approve political contributions of any kind.

Any solicitation of company employees for contributions to trade groups or other PAC interests must be approved by the organization's OGA. Likewise, contributions of the company's resources to charitable organizations must be approved by your corporate relations department.

CHARITABLE EVENTS

Rule: clear all charitable contributions of company funds and leadership positions in charitable events that may be associated with company business with your corporate communications department.

INTERNATIONAL BUSINESS AND THE FOREIGN CORRUPT PRACTICES ACT (FCPA)

For those of you working for international companies, there are certain specific rules that fall under the FCPA that you'll need to be aware of and adhere to. For example, employees or agents of your company may not make payments to foreign officials for an improper purpose. Such improper payments to foreign officials might include business courtesies or gifts to foreign officials. Similarly, no agreements may be entered into that call for the company to honor any boycott not sanctioned by the US government.

It is likewise illegal for any US company to undermine US government sanctions on certain countries or individuals. US embargoes and trade restrictions may be in effect with other nations at any given time (think Afghanistan, Iran, North Korea, and the like). Any prospective business activities with organizations designated as under trade restriction or embargo must be discussed with your company attorney before proceeding.

ENVIRONMENTAL SUSTAINABILITY AND CORPORATE SOCIAL RESPONSIBILITY

And don't forget this critical area of business ethics! This lends itself easily to multiple books, as there are so many areas in this topic that it's challenging to figure out where to begin. If you take a college course on ethics, you'll learn about the United Nations' seventeen Sustainable Development Goals intended to create a better, fairer world by addressing hunger, poverty, gender equality, access to education, clean water and sanitation, and decent work and economic growth. Similarly, the United Nations' Global Compact maps out the world's largest corporate sustainability initiatives. A quick Google search on these topics will open you to the world of ethics and sustainability for the twenty-first century organization, coupling business success with global community partnership.

As you can see, the implications of SOX and the broader field of ethics can be far reaching and complex. Just remember, when in doubt, escalate the matter to the appropriate executive above you. In other words, always be sure to "get the hot potato off your lap" in case anything goes wrong. Ethics revolves around transparency, and every organization relies on a practice of disclosure and review to resolve ethical challenges. Ethical quandaries are meant to be solved as a team sport. Further, when you escalate, you'll always be deemed to be working within the course and scope of your employment, which protects your job and eliminates any personal liability that might otherwise come your way.

THE FUTURE OF WORKPLACE ETHICS

As long as there's a business world, ethical quandaries will surely come your way. Thinking back over the past few decades, we've faced stock market highs that came crashing down, pandemics, impeachments, the ugly effects of global warming, the outright elimination of certain industries and jobs, and so much more. Change feels like it's coming faster than ever. While we can't know what's around the next corner, we can remain abreast of the current hot items that will likely impact our organizations and our careers in the near future. Here are three examples to ponder as we end our book journey together.

GENDER PARITY

The subject of wage inequality between the sexes remains a contentious topic, although it has been more than fifty years since the Equal Pay Act (1963) and the Civil Rights Act (1964) were passed. According to the Bureau of Labor Statistics, the median salary for women is about 24 percent less than that of the median male salary—women earn 82 percent of what men earn. Although this wage disparity has decreased since the late 1970s—when it was 62 percent—it reflects the long road to realizing fully equal pay in the workplace. The disparity is even greater for Black and Hispanic women. Black women earn sixty-four cents and Hispanic women earn fifty-six cents to the dollar earned by white, non-Hispanic men.

The 1963 Equal Pay Act is still intact as the foundational principle surrounding gender pay equity, but it has found new momentum as of late. The Lilly Ledbetter Fair Pay Act of 2009 amended the statute of limitations for wage discrimination claims. The Paycheck Fairness Act was introduced in 2017 as a bill to amend the Fair Labor Standards Act of 1938 and introduce procedural protections to the Equal Pay Act of 1963 as part of an effort to provide more effective remedies to victims of wage discrimination based on gender differences. Over time, states like California introduced their own Paycheck Fairness Act and Equal Pay Act to strengthen the protections and enforcements that permeated the workplace for far too long, including prohibiting wage differences based on race and ethnicity. In 2018, asking salary history questions during the preemployment interview process was barred in an attempt to "blind the pay scales" of applicants' career histories, thus keeping prior salary history from perpetuating future incongruities in salary offers between males and females performing substantially similar work.

Is California setting the pace for the rest of the nation? Is California doing enough? Will your organization objectively review salary levels based on experience, education, and performance, regardless of gender, race, or ethnicity? Similarly, should every corporate board have at least one female member and/or one member of an ethnically protected class? How strongly do you feel about such disparities, and how far are you willing to go to proactively address them in your organization? Should these matters become strategic board initiatives?

JOBS FOR FELONS

Certain nonprofits focus on rehabilitating convicted felons by helping them find work once their sentences are completed. With the recidivism (that is, return-to-jail) rate so high for convicted felons who have nowhere to turn once they're back on the street upon release, nonprofits can step in to bridge the gap between employers looking to hire and recently released felons looking for work. Are corporations, as good corporate citizens, responsible for aiding those who recently completed their sentences? If so, to what degree and under what circumstances?

The nonprofits that focus on this area of human need assist in ex-felons' reintegration into society and help them find well-paying jobs and, potentially, career paths. They educate and train ex-felons to develop marketable skills. They market to companies the fact that there are "dishonesty bonds" offered by bonding programs that ex-felons can receive to assist them in getting hired and to put the employer at ease when considering hiring a former convict.

But companies perform stringent background checks and fingerprinting to minimize liability in the workplace. Until this movement gained momentum several years ago, employers did everything they could to avoid hiring anyone with a criminal record. The criminal record was typically used as the justification to bar employment under certain circumstances (although employers are required to state in employment applications that arrests are not necessarily bars to employment). The employer's logic has always been that if an employer either knew or should have known that a new hire's background posed potential danger to coworkers and the newly hired ex-felon committed some kind of crime, the company could be sued for negligent hiring and/or negligent retention.

How do you feel about the matter? Are companies morally and ethically responsible for hiring ex-felons? Would your company consider making such a hire? Would the dishonesty bonds mentioned above be enough to convince your CEO or head of legal affairs that hiring an ex-felon is worth the risk?

ARTIFICIAL INTELLIGENCE

Ethical challenges will continue to come our way for many reasons, but none more than due to the meteoric changes in technology. Artificial intelligence (AI) affects workplace ethics and captures more time in the media than just about anything else, and for good reason: most HR execs believe that harnessing this information is critical to organizational growth and development, but even more will tell you that they don't truly understand how to manage the "unintended consequences" of skewed data.

Ethics issues surrounding AI for HR represent the future of HR but are a real risk if not handled correctly. Everything from recruitment to workforce planning to performance management will be captured by AI technology in one form or another: cognitive technology, machine learning, and robotic-process automation (RPA) represent the very best tools available to measure human capital as a true corporate asset.

But there can be a "dark side" of "unintended consequences" if the data is skewed or biased, and legal claims of disparate impact or disparate treatment may result in class action litigation if employers aren't careful. What makes this even more challenging is that the majority of HR professionals aren't schooled in the evaluation of data analytics, don't know how algorithms work, and report that they don't have the technical acumen to evaluate these new, growing technologies. Consider:

▪ A company reported that it wished to "scrape internal communications data" using AI to gauge employee sentiment.

It found that an employee reported to a peer that she felt she was being harassed by a supervisor. What is the company's moral and ethical obligation to intercede when the information was communicated confidentially?

■ An investment banking firm developed a "success recruitment profile" algorithm that focused on matching the talents of its highest performers to applicants sourced on its Applicant Tracking System (ATS). All recommended results—100 percent—excluded female applicants from consideration.

Ethical Implications:

■ What is the appropriate ethical use of the data?
■ How can employers ensure that data remains bias-free and ethically acquired?
■ How does HR embrace a mindset of perpetual reinvention and digital enablement as part of its core capabilities?

The key: AI should be leveraged to *augment* the human experience—not *replace* it.

In other words, human analysis *and* AI must work together to identify commonsense limitations to the data being generated. AI isn't intended to a be a one-size-fits-all magical solution to all of our problems. Instead, it should be viewed as an enhancement tool to identify issues that might otherwise get missed. Embrace new technology but ensure that your HR team remains diligent for unintended consequences that should require you to redefine the criteria you're using so you can generate bias-free results.

Said another way, AI cannot make decisions for us, thus fostering dependency; the key is to promote these skills in humanity, helping us to become independent moral decision makers in our own right.

The flip side is to make sure we do not become vulnerable to what's known as *moral de-skilling,* where human beings delegate their decision-making capacity to technology, thereby weakening their ability to make morally sound decisions. Ethics cannot be set on autopilot, whether relying on technology to help manage company talent or discerning real from fake news, for example. Knowledge that is not practiced is lost. Moral development requires practice. Ethical "muscle" must be honed and developed over time and not relegated to a machine, no matter how tempting or appealing the possibility. Each of these three large-scale issues deserves its own in-depth study. Just keep in mind that as long as human beings attempt to shortcut systems and find loopholes, there will be ethical quandaries and consequences that come your way.

▪ ▪ ▪

I hope this book did its part in increasing your awareness about the potential impact that ethical challenges might have on the organizations where you work as well as on your own personal career and professional development. The greatest investment you can make in yourself lies in developing a reputation as an ethical and moral business leader and human being. Make ethics the primary driver of your leadership brand, and everything else will surely align itself and fall into place. Thank you for allowing me to walk this path with you, pointing out the many benefits and opportunities that selfless, ethical leadership holds for you as you grow and develop in your own career. Now it's time for you to apply this wisdom, model this mindset, and pay it forward to grow leaders who follow in your ethical and moral footsteps.

ACKNOWLEDGMENTS

My heartfelt thanks to Professor Jeffrey Thies, director of the Institute for Business Ethics and Sustainability at Loyola Marymount University in Los Angeles, for his detailed guidance and recommendations in helping me identify and explore the key issues and drivers behind ethics in the workplace. And to an outstanding legal duo for being so selfless with their time and attention to select portions of this manuscript: Adam Rosenthal, partner and employment law attorney, author, and lecturer on HR law and compliance, and Kristin Housh, partner and business and securities law litigation attorney, both in the Del Mar (San Diego) office of Sheppard Mullin Richter & Hampton, LLP.

I can't thank you all enough for the time and attention you so selflessly shared in making this book a reality.

INDEX

ABOUT THE AUTHOR

Paul Falcone (www.PaulFalconeHR.com) is the chief human resources officer (CHRO) of the Motion Picture and Television Fund in Woodland Hills, California, where he's responsible for all aspects of HR leadership and strategy. He's the former CHRO of the Nickelodeon Animation Studios and head of international human resources for Paramount Pictures in Hollywood. Paul served as head of HR for the TV production unit of NBC-Universal, where he oversaw HR operations for NBC's late night and primetime programming lineup, including *The Tonight Show*, *Saturday Night Live*, and *The Office*. Paul is a renowned expert on effective interviewing and hiring, performance management, and leadership development, especially in terms of helping companies build higher-performing leadership teams. He also has extensive experience in healthcare/biotech and financial services across international, nonprofit, and union environments.

Paul is the author of a number of HarperCollins Leadership, AMACOM, and SHRM books, many of which have been ranked on Amazon as #1 bestsellers in the areas of human resources management, labor and employment law, business mentoring and coaching, communication in management, and business decision-making and problem-solving. Bestselling books like *101 Tough Conversations to Have with Employees*, *101 Sample Write-Ups for Documenting Employee Performance Problems*, and

96 Great Interview Questions to Ask Before You Hire have been translated into Chinese, Vietnamese, Korean, Indonesian, and Turkish.

Paul is a certified executive coach through the Marshall Goldsmith Stakeholder Centered Coaching program, a long-term contributor to SHRM.org and *HR Magazine*, and an adjunct faculty member in UCLA Extension's School of Business and Management, where he's taught courses on workplace ethics, recruitment and selection, legal aspects of human resources management, and international human resources. He is an accomplished keynote presenter, inhouse trainer, and webinar facilitator in the areas of talent management and effective leadership communication.